中国文化元典文选

The Selected Canons of Chinese Culture

（中英双语）

主　编　李孝英　赵彦春
副主编　邝旖雯　冯智娇

西南交通大学出版社
·成　都·

图书在版编目（CIP）数据

中国文化元典文选：汉、英 / 李孝英，赵彦春主编
. 一成都：西南交通大学出版社，2022.11
ISBN 978-7-5643-9017-4

Ⅰ. ①中… Ⅱ. ①李… ②赵… Ⅲ. ①中华文化－高
等学校－教材－汉、英 Ⅳ. ①K203

中国版本图书馆 CIP 数据核字（2022）第 216532 号

Zhongguo Wenhua Yuandian Wenxuan (Zhongying Shuangyu)
中国文化元典文选（中英双语）
主编 李孝英 赵彦春

责任编辑 赵玉婷
封面设计 原谋书装

出版发行 西南交通大学出版社
（四川省成都市金牛区二环路北一段 111 号
西南交通大学创新大厦 21 楼）
发行部电话 028-87600564 028-87600533
邮政编码 610031
网址 http://www.xnjdcbs.com
印刷 成都中永印务有限责任公司
成品尺寸 170 mm × 230 mm
印张 14.25
字数 291 千
版次 2022 年 11 月第 1 版
印次 2022 年 11 月第 1 次
书号 ISBN 978-7-5643-9017-4
定价 49.00 元

前言 Preface

习近平主席在 2021 年 5 月 31 日就加强我国国际传播能力建设进行主持学习时强调“讲好中国故事，传播好中国声音，展示真实、立体、全面的中国，是加强我国国际传播能力建设的重要任务”。同时，他指出“要更好推动中华文化走出去，以文载道、以文传声、以文化人，向世界阐释推介更多具有中国特色、体现中国精神、蕴藏中国智慧的优秀文化”。中华优秀文化的传承和发展以及国家发展战略需要我们深入而准确地阐释中国元典中蕴藏的中国智慧，深入挖掘和梳理中华优秀传统文化的发生、发展以及历史根源，尤其关注中华优秀传统文化的科学精神，惟其如此才能真正向世界阐释推介具有中国特色的科学智慧，体现中国文化的科学精神。中华民族历来对人类自然和社会就有“为天地立心，为生民立命，为往圣继绝学，为万世开太平”的责任和担当。

本书立足于国家战略，革新以往仅以汉语形式展现给我国研究生及中国文化爱好者的国学内容。研究生不但要自己知晓中国文化经典，还要学会向西方人准确介绍中国文化。提升研究生灵活运用本土语言和英语的能力，使其懂得用英语表达中国文化经典，这是新文科背景下，研究生文化老师们应积极面对的大事。基于此，本人和中国典籍翻译家赵彦春教授商议决定编写《中国文化元典文选（中英双语）》这本书。目前国内同类教材并不多见，这也是本团队编写这本书的动因之一。关于“元典”概念，读者可参见李建中编写的《中国文化：元典与要义》（北京师范大学出版社 2016 年版），在此不再赘述。本书受西南交通大学研究生教材（专著）经费建设项目（项目编号：SWJTU-JC2022-011）专项资助，特此致谢！

21 世纪以来，中国历史进入了新的转型时期，经济快速发展，文化日渐繁荣，亦趋向传统文化的回归。然而，文化的回归不是对传统文化的简单重复，而是从传统文化中汲取灵感，以获取前进的动力。本书选取了中国文化元典中最为精粹的内容，为目标语读者获取中国文化精髓提供了便利，也为当代读者寻找中国智慧之源提供指导。本书的主要特点如下：

第一，本书以中国文化元典（如《论语》《孟子》《道德经》《庄子》《墨子》《韩非子》及古典诗歌等）为主要内容，以中华文化传播与交流为宗旨，以实现中华文化精髓的传承与发扬为目的。

第二，本书精心挑选中国文化元典中的经典篇目，以双语对照形式编排。其英文译者是我国著名的典籍翻译家赵彦春教授，他翻译的诸多中国文化经典受到海内外读者的高度评价，如中华文化海外传播的"拳头产品"《英韵三字经》等。他博学广识，深谙中国文化经典之精髓，又综合考量译入语读者的审美旨趣，其译文是中华文化海外传播的佳品。

第三，本书用汉语和英语双语呈现，既增长学生的中国古典文化知识，又提升其英语水平，让读者在学习中国古典文化的同时，领略中西方语言和思维方式的差异性。

本书共九章，涉及中国古典文学、史学、经学、儒家、道家、墨家、法家、兵家和佛家的诸多文化元典，选取各领域最为经典的篇目或语段，以中英文对照形式呈现给目标读者。这不仅有利于在课堂教学中引入中国文化元典的内容，也能让读者精准快速地获取中华文化精髓，感受中华文化的无限魅力。本书覆盖面非常广，按照中华文化经典内在的蕴含进行整合与梳理，从文学、历史、经学、儒学、道学、兵学和佛学等视角揭示中华文化之精神要义，使读者在了解中华精神来源的同时，弄清中华民族文化的来龙去脉，从而更为深刻地认识文化元典的历史价值和现代意义。本书适用于中国高校本科生、研究生的中国文化通识教育，英语或翻译专业学生的汉英翻译和跨文化交际，海外孔子学院的中国文化课教学等课程，亦可作为中国高校留学生学习中国文化元典的重要工具书等。

此外，本书还可以作为中国文化海外传播的重要途径，双语对照排版模式为译入语读者提供了便捷的文化知识窗口，有助于扩大海外读者群体，提升中国文化元典海外知名度。

中华文化历经数千年，源远流长。中华古典文化形式多样、风格各异，有着自身独有的精神脉络和审美意趣。自有文字始，中华民族对文化的追求历久弥新，并保持着旺盛的生命力。本书第一章以中华古典文学为起点，逐步走进中华民族的精神世界。中国是诗歌的国度，第一节聚焦于中国第一部诗歌总集《诗经》，从中国诗歌之滥觞看古朴与典雅的结合，探中华风雅之起源。第二节呈现楚辞华彩，领略骚体新风，体会横跨千年的深情与烈骨。第三节选自《文心雕龙》开篇《原道》，为该书理论基础，涉及文德、文采、文史、文质之论，开文思之先河，成艺理之大观。第四、五节着眼于中国古典诗歌的巅峰——唐诗，以大唐诗坛双子星的作品为万花筒，看李白自然天成、率真酣畅的浪漫抒发，见杜甫忧国忧民、浑厚苍劲的理性表达，察乐府、古体、近体诗歌的多元体裁、题材，窥格律从无到有、经随意而谨严的流变。本章通过对中华古典文学史上部分扛鼎之作的翻译，力图跨语言、跨文化地展现中华古典文学的璀璨辉煌。译文尤其尊重古典诗歌的形式要求，以类比的方式还原汉诗韵律的风采，惟愿以此为中华文化的国际传播提供样例。

华夏文明滥觞于上古，从文字产生以来历史记载从未间断。“以史为鉴可以知兴替”，中国史学整合了历史、科学、哲学、人性、政治等多方面内容。第二章按照时间顺序节选中国史学上重要文献的经典论述，管窥史家的德识才学。第一节从中国第一部较为完备的编年史《左传》的双语对照入手为读者展示春秋时期周室衰微、诸侯争霸的历史碎片和礼仪、典章、伦理、民族、神话等社会内容的记述和评论。第二节是对中国第一部纪传体通史《史记》的节选，该书以人物传记为中心，包罗了从黄帝时代到汉武帝时期政治、军事、经济、文化等各方面的发展状况；本节以双语形式带领读者读太史公如何“究天人之际，通古今之变，成一家之言”。《汉书》为中国第一部纪传体断代史，从《史记》到《汉书》展现了儒家思想在汉代成为正统的演变过程，第三节部分呈现《汉书》的历史材料。汉代之后的大一统政权为唐朝，第四节节选该时期的政论性史书《贞观政要》，包含魏征、杜如晦、房玄龄等大臣在君臣和军政问题上的争议、劝谏和奏议等。第五节则节选了中国第一部编年体通史《资治通鉴》的内容，用汉英双语再现司马光对政治、军事、民族关系政策的观点。史书中喜用古语古词，读之艰涩，译文部分则在保留原文风格的基础上，更为清晰地传达了原文要义。

早期儒家以《诗》《书》《礼》《乐》《易》《春秋》为六经，后世又发展为十三经（《易经》《尚书》《诗经》《周礼》《仪礼》《礼记》《春秋左传》《春秋公羊传》《春秋穀梁传》《孝经》《论语》《孟子》《尔雅》）。经董仲舒的努力，儒学成为官学，而经学也就成为中华传统思想核心的重要载体。第三章为经学，摘取《周易》和《尚书》的重要论述，探索中华核心思想的来源。译文特别遵循了《周易》"取象比类"的思维模式，凸显中华传统认知的特点；《尚书》中佶屈聱牙的文辞转换成英文后既保留了原文的简洁之风，又更易于理解。

儒家是起源于中国并影响及流传至周边东亚国家的文化主流思想与教派体系。第四章为儒家元典作品的节选，选取儒家代表作《论语》《孟子》以及《孝经》中经典篇目，以彰显儒家学说之经世致用思想及开放包容的情怀。孔子作为儒家学派的创始人，在《论语》第一节中阐释了仁、义、礼、智、信的伦理思想，对中国乃至全世界都产生了深远的影响。孟子是战国时期的哲学家、思想家和教育家，与孔子并称为"孔孟"。第二节《孟子》是总结战国时期各国治乱兴亡规律的作品，其中的"民为贵，社稷次之，君为轻"的观点对后世君王的治国理政具有重要的启示价值。第三节《孝经》为儒家孝道伦理方面的经典之作，是儒家十三经之一。《孝经》将"孝"看作人性伦理之规范，"夫孝，天之经也，地之义也，人之行也"。可见，孝是人类德行之本，上至国君，下至臣民都应以孝规约自身，由己及人。译文采用异化处理策略，紧贴原文，以求还原儒家思想之真实样貌，让译入语读者感知儒学的博大精深。

道家以"道"为核心，主张大道无为、道法自然，具有朴素的辩证法思想。第五章选取了道家文化元典《道德经》和《庄子》中的经典篇目。《道德经》为春秋时期老子所作，是道家哲学思想的重要来源，全书共计八十一篇。第一节选取其中十八篇，展现《道德经》中"内圣外王"之学，以期为后世学者提供道家哲学的精神滋养。《庄子》是道家哲学的另一部力作，包括内篇、外篇和杂篇，内篇被认为由庄子本人所著，是庄子思想的核心。第二节选取了内篇之《逍遥游》《齐物论》和《养生主》三篇。《逍遥游》作为《庄子》全书总纲，突显了庄子以“至人无己，神人无功，圣人无名”的态度来阐释道家生命哲学之奥秘，进而企及无限逍遥的哲学境界。庄子在《齐物论》中提倡齐一万物，无是非分别，表现了庄子对世俗的否定以及对自由境界的无限向往。庄子在《养生主》中指出养生须秉承事物中虚之道，顺应自然的变化与发展，为现世读者的生活与生存之道带来启迪。译文以娴熟流畅的语言、整齐划一的形式、灵动优美的韵律再现了道家哲学之崇尚自然、清净无为，追求自由的生命境界。

春秋战国时期的百家争鸣有“非儒即墨”的提法，足以见得墨家思想之时代价值。第六章为墨家代表作品《墨子》的篇目选辑。墨子在这部著作中提倡兼爱、非攻、尚贤、尚同、非命、非乐等思想，涉及政治学、逻辑学、军事学、几何学等领域，尤以逻辑思想最为突出，是先秦逻辑学的集大成者。本章选取了《兼爱》《尚贤》《非攻》《尚同》《七患》等篇目来映现墨子的“非攻”“爱民”“兼爱”等“爱利百姓”思想，突出墨子以“兴天下大利，除天下之害”为己任的崇高理想。译文以通俗易懂的句式结构和语言表达准确传达了墨学思想之精义和内涵，希冀后世学者能以一斑而窥全豹，深刻感知墨家学派的思想精髓。

法家是我国历史上提倡以法治为核心的重要学派，是战国末期平民百姓的政治代言人，在政治上可谓是“独步天下”。第七章是我国法家思想之集大成者韩非子的作品选辑。法家经典《韩非子》将“国无常强，无常弱。奉法者强，则国强；奉法者弱，则国弱”作为君主专制的基本思想，秉持历史发展观，主张极端的功利主义，强调以法治国，以利用人，是中国封建社会领导阶层的统治法宝。《韩非子》由五十五篇论文集辑而成，本章选取其中十八篇，以汉英对照的形式向后世学者展现韩非子的历史进步论、朴素辩证法以及改革与法治等观点，使法家元典学习与文化传播紧密融合。

兵学在中国文化发展中有着源远流长的历史，兵学产生于西周，成熟于春秋，是我国传统文化中的军事瑰宝。诸子百家之一的兵家经典体现了中国古代军事思想之要旨。第八章选取《孙子兵法》《孙膑兵法》以及《吴子》等中的部分篇目，向当代学子揭示“兵者，国之大事，死生之地，存亡之道，不可不察也”的中国古代军事思想精粹。兵学元典《孙子兵法》《孙膑兵法》以及《吴子》等均以博大精深的内容、深邃玄妙的思想、缜密严谨的逻辑而著称于世，是我国古代军事文化的璀璨明珠，是当代学子必读的中国兵学思想佳作。译文以原文为纲，综合考量目标读者的审美旨趣和阅读习惯，将中国兵家文化精髓以简洁凝练的句法结构、通俗易懂的文字表达再现出来，以期提升我国兵学典籍的跨语境传播效果。

早在东汉时期，佛教便传入中国，随着宗教文化的传播与变迁，形成了独具东方文化特色的中国佛教，与儒教和道教一同构筑了中国传统文化的三大精神支柱。第九章为佛家思想的经典选辑，展现了佛家禅语之精妙，如世人耳熟能详的四句偈语“菩提本无树，明镜亦非台，本来无一物，何处惹尘埃”旨在揭示世间一切皆如梦幻泡影，劝导世人摆脱虚妄执着，才能明心见性，自证菩提。本章选取的《菩提本无树》《无量寿经》《四十二章经》以及《阿弥陀经》等都是佛家遗响千年的经典作品。译文以简洁精当的语言向目标读者展示佛家智慧之精微玄妙，彰显出中国佛学文化的无限魅力。

中华民族历经五千年，沉淀了惠泽万世的璀璨华夏文明和文化。党和国家一贯重视增强中华文化国际影响力，主推中华文化经典作品的外译。中国文化元典荟萃先民智慧，其思想富于原创性，其主题具有恒久性。中国文化元典涵盖后世中华文化的各类文化因子，从历史的角度而言，决定了中华文化发展的方向及文化特性。

目录 Contents

第一章　文学 ········ 001

Chapter I　Literature ········ 001

第一节　《诗经》 ········ 001

Section 1　*The Book of Songs* ········ 001

1. 关雎　The Grebes Coo ········ 001
2. 桃夭　The Peach ········ 002
3. 击鼓　War Drums ········ 002
4. 式微　It's Dark ········ 003
5. 黍离　Millet Droops Low ········ 004
6. 子衿　Your Blue Collar ········ 005
7. 蒹葭　The Reeds ········ 005
8. 无衣　No Clothes ········ 006
9. 蜉蝣　Ephemeron ········ 007
10. 鹿鸣　The Deer Bleat ········ 008
11. 常棣　Cherry Blossoms ········ 009
12. 采薇　Vetch We Pick ········ 010

第二节　《楚辞》 ········ 012

Section 2　*Ch'u Verse* ········ 012

1. 离骚（节选）Woebegone (excerpt) ········ 012

2. 少司命（节选） Life God Junior (excerpt) ········· 015
3. 惜往日（节选）Missing the Bygone Day (excerpt) ········· 016
4. 橘颂 Ode to the Orange ········· 016
5. 天问（节选）Asking the Sky (excerpt) ········· 019
6. 渔父 The Fisherman ········· 021
第三节 《文心雕龙》 ········· 024
Section 3 *Carve the Dragon with Your Literary Heart* ········· 024
1. 原道 Back to the Word ········· 024
第四节 李白诗歌 ········· 025
Section 4 Pai Li's Poems ········· 025
1. 静夜思 Night Thought ········· 025
2. 清平调（其一）Pure Peace Tune, No.1 ········· 026
3. 峨眉山月歌 A Song of the Moon o'er Mt. Brow ········· 026
4. 黄鹤楼送孟浩然之广陵 Seeing off Haojan Meng to Broadridge at Yellow Crane Tower ········· 027
5. 宣州谢朓楼饯别校书叔云 Seeing Off Yün, My Uncle, a Collator, on T'iao Hsieh's Tower in Hsuan ········· 027
6. 长相思 Long Longing ········· 028
7. 赠汪伦 To Lun Wang ········· 029
8. 上李邕 To Yung Li ········· 030
9. 将进酒 Do Drink Wine ········· 031
10. 蜀道难 The Shu Way Is Hard ········· 033
第五节 杜甫诗歌 ········· 037
Section 5 Fu Tu's Poems ········· 037
1. 春望 A View of Spring ········· 037
2. 赠花卿 To Hua, a General ········· 038
3. 月夜忆舍弟 Missing My Brothers on a Moonlit Night ········· 038

4. 旅夜书怀 Traveling at Night …… 039
5. 客至 A Friend's Visit …… 040
6. 望岳 Looking at Mt. Arch …… 040
7. 春夜喜雨 A Blessing Rain on a Spring Night …… 041
8. 饮中八仙歌 Song of Eight Drinking Immortals …… 042
9. 兵车行 The Chariot: A Ballad …… 044
第二章 史学 …… 048
Chapter Ⅱ History …… 048
第一节 《左传》 …… 048
Section 1 *Tso's Annals* …… 048
1. 隐公十一年 The Eleventh Year Under Lord Yin …… 048
2. 桓公十二年 The Twelve Year Under Lord Column …… 048
3. 庄公二十四年 The Twenty-Fourth Year of Lord Chuang …… 049
4. 僖公五年 The Fifth Year Under Lord Hsi …… 049
5. 僖公九年 The Ninth Year Under Lord Hsi …… 049
6. 僖公十三年 The Thirteenth Year Under Lord Hsi …… 049
7. 僖公十四年 The Fourteenth Year Under Lord Hsi …… 049
8. 文公六年 The Sixth Year of Lord Civil …… 050
9. 文公十三年 The Thirteen Year of Lord Civil …… 051
10. 文公十六年 The Sixteen Year Under Lord Civil …… 051
11. 宣公二年 The Second Year of Lord Clare …… 051
12. 宣公十二年 The Twelfth Year of Lord Clare …… 051
13. 宣公十五年 The Fifteenth Year of Lord Clare …… 052
14. 成公二年 The Second Year Under Lord Ch'eng …… 052
15. 成公十二年 The Twelve Year Under Lord Ch'eng …… 052
16. 成公十五年 The Fifteenth Year Under Lord Ch'eng …… 052
17. 成公十六年 The Sixteenth Year Under Lord Ch'eng …… 053

18. 襄公十年 The Tenth Year of Lord Hsiang ········· 053
19. 襄公十一年 The Eleventh Year of Lord Hsiang ········· 053
20. 襄公十三年 The Thirteen Year of Lord Hsiang ········· 053
21. 襄公二十二年 The Twenty-Second Year of Lord Hsiang ········· 054
22. 襄公二十五年 The Twenty-Fifth Year of Lord Hsiang ········· 054
23. 襄公二十九年 The Twenty-Ninth Year of Lord Hsiang ········· 054
24. 襄公三十年 The Thirtieth Year of Lord Hsiang ········· 054
25. 昭公四年 The Forth Year Under Lord Glare ········· 054
26. 昭公五年 The Forth Year Under Lord Glare ········· 055
27. 昭公十年 The Tenth Year Under Lord Glare ········· 055
28. 昭公二十年 The Twentieth Year Under Lord Glare ········· 055
29. 昭公二十五年 The Twenty-Fifth Year Under Lord Glare ········· 055
30. 哀公元年 The First Year of Lord Sad ········· 056
31. 哀公七年 The Seventh Year of Lord Sad ········· 056
32. 春秋左传正义・昭公六年 Commentary on *Tso's Annals*: The Sixth Year Under Lord Glare ········· 056
33. 春秋左传正义・昭公二十九年 Commentary on *Tso's Annals*: The Twenty-Ninth Year Under Lord Glare ········· 057

第二节 《史记》 ········· 057

Section 2 *Records of the Grand Historian* ········· 057

1. 五帝本纪 Records of the Five Lords ········· 057
2. 殷本纪 Records of Yin ········· 059
3. 秦始皇本纪 Records of Emperor First of Ch'in ········· 059
4. 高祖本纪 Records of Pang Liu, Highroot of Han ········· 059
5. 货殖列传 Biography of Merchants ········· 061
6. 商君列传 Biography of Yang Shang ········· 062
7. 循吏列传 Biography of Good Officials ········· 063

8. 酷吏列传 Biography of Cruel Officials ······························ 064
9. 屈原贾生列传 Biography of Yüan Ch'ü and E Chia ················ 065
10. 日者列传 Biography of Augurs ··· 065
11. 淮阴侯列传 Marquess of IIuaishadc ···································· 065
12. 齐悼惠王世家 Aristocratic Family of Prince
Mournboon of Ch'i··· 065
13. 赵世家 Aristocratic Family of Chao ···································· 066
14. 楚世家 Aristocratic Family of Ch'u ····································· 066
15. 楚元王世家 Aristocratic Family of King One of Ch'u ·············· 066
16. 曹相国世家 Aristocratic Family of Premier Ts'ao ·················· 066
17. 礼书 Rites ·· 067
18. 太史公自序 Grand Historiographer's Preface ························ 067
第三节 《汉书》 ·· 067
Section 3 *The History of Han*·· 067
1. 景帝纪 Record of Emperor Scene ······································ 067
2. 食货志 Foods and Goods ·· 068
3. 陈胜项籍传 Biography of Sheng Ch'en and Chi Hsiang ············ 068
4. 楚元王传 Biography of Chiao Liu, First Prince of Ch'u············ 068
5. 张释之传 Biography of Shihchih Chang ······························· 069
6. 董仲舒传 Biography of Chungshu Tung ······························· 069
7. 王褒传 Biography of Pao Wang ·· 070
8. 杨胡朱梅云传 Biography of Wangsun Yang, Chien Hu,
Yün Chu, Fu Mei, and Ch'ang Yün ···································· 070
9. 陈汤传 Biography of T'ang Ch'en··································· 070
10. 王贡两龚鲍传 Biography of Chi Wang, Yü Kung,
Sheng Kung, She Kung and Hsuan Pao································ 070
11. 宣元六王传 Biography of Six Kings under the Reigns of
Emperor Piousbroad and Emperor Piousfirst of Han ················ 071

12. 傅喜传 Biography of Hsi Fu ··· 071
第四节 《贞观政要》 ··· 071
Section 4 *Governance of Right Done* ··· 071
1. 君道 Sovereignty ··· 071
2. 政体 Governance ··· 073
3. 附：直谏 Admonishment ··· 076
4. 君臣鉴戒 Commandments for the Emperor and Officials ··· 076
5. 择官 Appointment ··· 076
6. 规谏太子 Admonishing a Crown Prince ··· 078
7. 公平 Fairness ··· 079
8. 慎所好 Caution in Interest ··· 080
9. 慎言语 Caution in Speech ··· 081
10. 悔过 Repentance ··· 082
11. 崇儒学 Admiring Confucianism ··· 082
12. 务农 Agriculture ··· 083
13. 征伐 Expedition ··· 083
第五节 《资治通鉴》 ··· 084
Section 5 *History as a Mirror* ··· 084
1. 周纪一 The First Volume of the Records of Chough ··· 084
2. 周纪二 The Second Volume of the Records of Chough ··· 084
3. 周纪四 The Forth Volume of the Records of Chough ··· 085
4. 秦纪二 The Second Volume of the Records of Ch'in ··· 086
5. 汉纪三 The Third Volume of the Records of Han ··· 086
6. 汉纪九 The Ninth Volume of the Records of Han ··· 086
7. 汉纪十 The Tenth Volume of the Records of Han ··· 087
8. 汉纪十一 The Eleventh Volume of the Records of Han ··· 087
9. 汉纪十六 The Sixteenth Volume of the Records of Han ··· 088

10. 汉纪十七 The Seventeenth Volume of the Records of Han ······· 088
11. 汉纪二十一 The Twenty-First Volume of the Records of the Han Dynasty ······· 088
12. 汉纪二十四 The Twenty-Forth Volume of the Records of Han ··· 089
13. 汉纪四十三 The Forty-Third Volume of the Records of Han ······ 089
14. 高祖武皇帝十五 Record of Lord Marshal, Highroot of Liang ···· 089
15. 唐纪二 The Second Volume of the Records of T'ang ······· 090
16. 唐纪八 The Eighth Volume of the Records of T'ang ······· 090
17. 唐纪十 The Tenth Volume of the Records of T'ang ······· 091
18. 唐纪五十 The Fiftieth Volume of the Records of T'ang ······· 091
第三章 经学 ······· 093
Chapter Ⅲ Confucian Classics ······· 093
第一节 《周易》 ······· 093
Section 1 *Changes* ······· 093
1. 系辞 Attribution ······· 093
2. 乾卦第一 Diagram 1: Gen ······· 096
3. 坤卦第二 Diagram 2: Kueen ······· 097
4. 需卦第五 Diagram 5: Need ······· 097
5. 泰卦第十一 Diagram 11: Tower ······· 097
6. 否卦第十二 Diagram 12: Obstacle ······· 098
7. 剥卦第二十三 Diagram 23: Spall ······· 098
8. 颐卦第二十七 Diagram 27: Ease ······· 098
9. 明夷卦第三十六 Diagram 36: Archery ······· 098
10. 损卦第四十一 Diagram 41: Wane ······· 098
11. 震卦第五十一 Diagram 51: Thunder ······· 098
12. 艮卦第五十二 Diagram 52: Choke ······· 099
13. 丰卦第五十五 Diagram 55: Harvest ······· 099

14. 中孚卦第六十一 Diagram 61: Integrity …… 099
15. 序卦 Order …… 099
第二节 《尚书》 …… 100
Section 2 *High Book* …… 100
1. 尧典 Record of Lord Mound …… 100
2. 洪范 Universal Norms …… 104
3. 皋陶谟 Moor Potter's Counsel …… 105
4. 牧誓 A Pledge at Muyeh …… 107
5. 商书 · 仲虺之诰 Book of Shang: Lizard's Admonition …… 107
6. 盘庚 Pankeng …… 107
7. 周书 · 泰誓 Book of Chough: Grand Pledge …… 108
8. 周书 · 周官 Book of Chough: Officials of Chough …… 108
9. 五子之歌 Songs of Five Lords …… 109
10. 康诰 Admonition to K'ang …… 109
第四章 儒家 …… 112
Chapter Ⅳ Confucianism …… 112
第一节 《论语》 …… 112
Section 1 *The Annalects* …… 112
1. 学而 Isn't It …… 112
2. 为政 Governing …… 116
3. 述而 Retelling But …… 121
第二节 《孟子》 …… 128
Section 2 *Mencius* …… 128
1. 告子 Sir Teller …… 128
2. 公孙丑上 Ugly Lordson (Upper) …… 129
3. 公孙丑下 Ugly Lordson (Lower) …… 130
4. 梁惠王上 King Boon of Liang (Upper) …… 131

5. 梁惠王下 King Boon of Liang (Lower) ······ 131
6. 尽心上 Heart and Soul (Upper) ······ 133
7. 尽心下 Heart and Soul (Lower) ······ 133
第三节 《孝经》 ······ 134
Section 3 *Filial Piety* ······ 134
1. 开宗明义 Introduction ······ 134
2. 圣治 Ruling the World with Filial Piety ······ 134
3. 三才 Three Vitals ······ 134
4. 广扬名 Ever-lasting Fame ······ 135
5. 谏诤 Remonstrance ······ 135
6. 五刑 Five Punishments ······ 136
第五章 道家 ······ 137
Chapter Ⅴ Wordism (Taoism) ······ 137
第一节 《道德经》 ······ 137
Section 1 *The Word and the World* ······ 137
1. 第一篇 Chapter Ⅰ ······ 137
2. 第二篇 Chapter Ⅱ ······ 137
3. 第五篇 Chapter Ⅴ ······ 138
4. 第八篇 Chapter Ⅷ ······ 138
5. 第九篇 Chapter Ⅸ ······ 138
6. 第十二篇 Chapter XII ······ 139
7. 第二十三篇 Chapter XXIII ······ 139
8. 第二十五篇 Chapter XXV ······ 140
9. 第二十八篇 Chapter XXVIII ······ 140
10. 第三十三篇 Chapter XXXIII ······ 141
11. 第四十二篇 Chapter XXXXII ······ 141
12. 第四十五篇 Chapter XXXXV ······ 141

13. 第四十八篇 Chapter XXXXVIII …… 142
14. 第六十六篇 Chapter LXVI …… 142
15. 第六十七篇 Chapter LXVII …… 142
16. 第七十一篇 Chapter LXXI …… 143
17. 第七十八篇 Chapter LXXVIII …… 143
18. 第八十篇 Chapter LXXX …… 143
第二节 《庄子》 …… 144
Section 2 *Sir Lush* …… 144
1. 逍遥游第一 Chapter Ⅰ: Flying Free …… 144
2. 齐物论第二 Chapter Ⅱ: Identified as One …… 150
3. 养生主第三 Chapter Ⅲ: Sustaining Life …… 164
第六章 墨家 …… 168
Chapter VI Inkism …… 168
第一节 《墨子·兼爱》 …… 168
Section 1 *Loving Others · Sir Ink* …… 168
1. 兼爱上 Loving Others (Upper) …… 168
2. 兼爱中 Loving Others (Middle) …… 169
3. 兼爱下 Loving Others (Lower) …… 170
第二节 《墨子·尚贤》 …… 170
Section 2 *Respecting Sages · Sir Ink* …… 170
1. 尚贤上 Respecting Sages (Upper) …… 170
2. 尚贤中 Respecting Sages (Middle) …… 171
第三节 其他篇目 …… 172
Section 3 Other Articles …… 172
1. 非攻 No War …… 172
2. 七患 Seven Dangers …… 173
3. 天志 Heaven's Will …… 174

4. 尚同 Alignment with Superiors ············ 175
5. 辞过 Criticism of Negligence ············ 176
6. 节用 Saving ············ 176
7. 亲士 Appointing Talents ············ 176
8. 修身 Character Cultivation ············ 176
9. 非乐 Prohibition of Music ············ 177
10. 贵义 Esteem for Righteousness ············ 177
11. 耕柱 Sir Tillpillar ············ 177
第七章 法家 ············ 178
Chapter VII Legalism ············ 178
第一节 《韩非子·解老》 ············ 178
Section 1 *Expounding Laocius · Sir Hanfei* ············ 178
1. 解老上 Expounding Laocius (Upper) ············ 178
2. 解老下 Expounding Laocius (Lower) ············ 179
第二节 其他篇目 ············ 180
Section 2 Other Articles ············ 180
1. 有度 Within a Limit ············ 180
2. 诡使 Deviation from the Right Path ············ 181
3. 难势 Difficult Situations ············ 181
4. 说疑 Explaining Doubts ············ 181
5. 内储说上七术 Seven Methods to Manage Subjects ············ 182
6. 五蠹 Five Types of Assholes ············ 182
7. 八经 Eight Eternal Rites ············ 182
8. 南面 Reigning ············ 183
9. 人主 Political Life ············ 183
10. 扬权 Enhancing Monarchial Power ············ 184
11. 亡征 Signs of a Dying Nation ············ 184

12. 显学 Famous Learning …… 185
13. 用人 Employing People …… 186
14. 大体 Overall Situation …… 186
15. 主道 The Way to Reign …… 186
16. 奸劫弑臣 Treacherous, Coercive, and Murderous Officials …… 187
第八章 兵家 …… 188
Chapter VIII Military Strategy …… 188
第一节 《孙子兵法》 …… 188
Section 1 *Wu Sun's Art of War* …… 188
1. 始计 Planning …… 188
2. 谋攻 Strategy …… 189
3. 九变 Nine Changes …… 190
4. 行军 Marching …… 190
5. 九地 Nine Places …… 191
6. 军争 Military Scramble …… 191
7. 地形 Topography …… 191
第二节 《孙膑兵法》 …… 192
Section 2 *Pin Sun's Art of War* …… 192
1. 篡卒 Picking of Valiant Soldiers …… 192
2. 行篡 Select Worthies …… 192
3. 见威王 An Audience with King Power …… 193
4. 八阵 Eight Battle Formations …… 193
第三节 《兵经·肃》 …… 194
Section 3 *Solemnity · Canons for War* …… 194
第四节 《吴子·图国》 …… 194
Section 4 *Governing the State · Ch'i Wu* …… 194
第五节 《尉缭子·战威》 …… 195
Section 5 *Power of War · Sir Weiliao* …… 195

第六节　《国语·越语下》…………………………………………… 195
Section 6　*Remarks of Yüeh · Remarks of the States* ………………… 195
第九章　佛家 ………………………………………………………… 197
Chapter IX　Buddhism ……………………………………………… 197
第一节　《菩提本无树》……………………………………………… 197
Section 1　*There's Nothing Like a Boddhi Tree* ……………………… 197
第二节　《无量寿经·歌叹佛德》……………………………………… 198
Section 2　*The Great Merits of Buddha · The Immortal Buddha* ………… 198
第三节　《四十二章经》……………………………………………… 199
Section 3　*The Buddha's Fourty-two Sutras* ………………………… 199
第四节　《阿弥陀经》………………………………………………… 200
Section 4　*Amitabha Sutras* ………………………………………… 200
第五节　《法句经·序》……………………………………………… 202
Section 5　Preface to *Dharmapada* …………………………………… 202
参考文献 …………………………………………………………… 204
References …………………………………………………………… 204

第一章　文学
Chapter I　Literature

第一节　《诗经》
Section 1　*The Book of Songs*

1. 关雎 The Grebes Coo

关关雎鸠，	Do-do, the grebes do coo
在河之洲。	At shoal amid the stream;
窈窕淑女，	The lad is keen to woo
君子好逑。	The lass, a virtuous dream.
参差荇菜，	Lush grows the water grass;
左右流之。	She picks it left and right.
窈窕淑女，	The lad would court the lass,
寤寐求之。	A-craving day and night.
求之不得，	No chance to win her hand,
寤寐思服。	Asleep, awake, he yearns.
悠哉悠哉，	Long night he cannot stand;
辗转反侧。	He tosses and he turns.
参差荇菜，	Lush grows the water grass;
左右采之。	She plucks it left and right.
窈窕淑女，	Lutes, flutes, do cheer the lass,
琴瑟友之。	Her interest to invite.

参差荇菜，	Lush grows the water grass;
左右芼之。	She culls it left and right.
窈窕淑女，	Bells, drums, do please the lass,
钟鼓乐之。	Her humor to delight.

2. 桃夭 The Peach

桃之夭夭，	The peach twigs sway,
灼灼其华。	Ablaze the flower;
之子于归，	Now she's married away,
宜其室家。	Befitting her new bower.
桃之夭夭，	The peach twigs sway,
有蕡其实。	Mellow the pome;
之子于归，	Now she's married away,
宜其家室。	Befitting her new home.
桃之夭夭，	The peach twigs sway,
其叶蓁蓁。	Verdant the frond,
之子于归，	Now she's married away,
宜其家人。	Befitting the folks fond.

3. 击鼓 War Drums

击鼓其镗，	Tang, tang, the war drums sound;
踊跃用兵。	The soldiers leap and bound.
土国城漕，	To build walls others stay;
我独南行。	Southward I make my way.

从孙子仲，	We follow him, Tsuchung,①
平陈与宋。	To appease Ch'en and Sung.
不我以归，	For long we can't go back;
忧心有忡。	How sad we are, alack!
爰居爰处？	Where to rest or abide?
爰丧其马？	Where is my horse to ride?
于以求之？	Where to find it, I brood;
于林之下。	I search and search the wood.
"死生契阔"，	"We'll never go apart"
与子成说。	The vow's borne in my heart.
执子之手，	Of your hands I took hold,
与子偕老。	"I'll stay with you till old."
于嗟阔兮，	We're kept far far away,
不我活兮。	When is our meeting day?
于嗟洵兮，	Apart for so long now,
不我信兮。	How can I keep the vow?

4. 式微 It's Dark

式微，式微，	It's dark, oh nearly black,
胡不归？	Why not go back?
微君之故，	If it's not for you, oh you,
胡为乎中露！	Why do we get wet with dew?

① Tsuchung: referring to Wenchung Lordson, with Tsuchung as his courtesy name, commander of the State of Wei. He once led the joint force of the States of Ch'en and Sung to attack the State of Cheng.

式微，式微，	It's dark, oh nearly black,
胡不归？	Why not go back?
微君之躬，	If it's not for you, esquire,
胡为乎泥中！	Why do we toil in the mire?

5. 黍离 Millet Droops Low

彼黍离离，	Millet with grain droops low;
彼稷之苗。	Sorghum attends the blade.
行迈靡靡，	So slowly I go through;
中心摇摇。	My heart is so dismayed.
知我者，谓我心忧；	He who knows me says I'm distraught.
不知我者，谓我何求。	He who doesn't asks if I'm seeking aught.
悠悠苍天，	O vast, almighty blue sky,
此何人哉！	Who on earth caused this and why?

彼黍离离，	Millet with grain droops low;
彼稷之穗。	Sorghum is in the ear.
行迈靡靡，	So slowly I go through;
中心如醉。	My heart feels drunk and drear.
知我者，谓我心忧；	He who knows me says I'm distraught.
不知我者，谓我何求。	He who doesn't asks if I'm seeking aught.
悠悠苍天，	O vast, almighty blue sky,
此何人哉！	Who on earth caused this and why?

彼黍离离，	Millet with grain droops low;
彼稷之实。	Sorghum is in the grain.
行迈靡靡，	So slowly I go through;

中心如噎。	My heart is choked with pain.
知我者，谓我心忧；	He who knows me says I'm distraught.
不知我者，谓我何求。	He who doesn't asks if I'm seeking aught.
悠悠苍天，	O vast, almighty blue sky,
此何人哉！	Who on earth caused this and why?

6. 子衿 Your Blue Collar

青青子衿，	You wear a collar blue;
悠悠我心。	Blue, blue, I think of you.
纵我不往，	Where you are I can't go,
子宁不嗣音？	Why no message to me, why no?
青青子佩，	A collar blue you wear;
悠悠我思。	Ware, ware, for you I care.
纵我不往，	Where you are I can't go,
子宁不来？	Why no sense of return, why no?
挑兮达兮，	Here nearby the gate tower,
在城阙兮。	I pace hour after hour.
一日不见，	One day that I miss you
如三月兮。	Is like three months ov'rdue.

7. 蒹葭 The Reeds

蒹葭苍苍，	The reeds sway, green and green;
白露为霜。	The white dew becomes frost.
所谓伊人，	The lady fair I mean
在水一方。	Looms yonder, all but lost.

溯洄从之， Upstream to her I row;
道阻且长。 The course is long and high.
溯游从之， Upstream to her I go;
宛在水中央。 On the waves she looks shy.

蒹葭凄凄， The reeds sway, clean and clean;
白露未晞。 The white dew has not dried.
所谓伊人， The lady fair I mean
在水之湄。 Looms by the riverside.
溯洄从之， Upstream to her I row;
道阻且跻。 The course is hard and high.
溯游从之， Upstream to her I go;
宛在水中坻。 On the strand she seems nigh.

蒹葭采采， The reeds sway, sheen and sheen;
白露未已。 The white dew as e'er gleams.
所谓伊人， The lady fair I mean
在水之涘。 Stands on the bank, it seems.
溯洄从之， Upstream to her I row;
道阻且右。 The course turns left and right.
溯游从之， Upstream to her I go;
宛在水中沚。 On the shoal she beams bright.

8. 无衣 No Clothes

岂曰无衣？ You have no clothes to wear?
与子同袍。 The same clothes we will share.
王于兴师， The Lord's bugle does flare!
修我戈矛， Let us make spear and shield,
与子同仇！ And go now to the field.

岂曰无衣？	You have no clothes to wear?
与子同泽。	The same shirt we will share.
王于兴师，	The Lord's bugle does flare!
修我矛戟，	Let us make lance and shield,
与子偕作！	And wend now to the field.
岂曰无衣？	You have no clothes to wear?
与子同裳。	The same gown we will share.
王于兴师，	The Lord's bugle does flare!
修我甲兵，	Let us make pike and shield,
与子偕行！	And march now to the field.

9. 蜉蝣 Ephemeron

蜉蝣之羽，	Ephemeron wings sheen
衣裳楚楚。	Like garments new and clean.
心之忧矣，	My heart is struck with care;
于我归处。	Where shall I go, o where?
蜉蝣之翼，	Ephemeron wings shine
采采衣服。	Like garments bright and fine.
心之忧矣，	My heart is struck with care;
于我归息。	Where shall I rest, o where?
蜉蝣掘阅，	Ephemerons take flight;
麻衣如雪。	Their sleek wings are snow white.
心之忧矣，	My heart is struck with care;
于我归说。	Where shall I die, o where?

10. 鹿鸣 The Deer Bleat

呦呦鹿鸣，	The deer each to each bleat;
食野之苹。	Afield wormwood they eat.
我有嘉宾，	I have good guests today;
鼓瑟吹笙。	The lute and flute we play.
吹笙鼓簧，	The reed and strings vibrate;
承筐是将。	I put gifts in the crate.
人之好我，	They are indeed good friends,
示我周行。	Showing me means and ends.
呦呦鹿鸣，	The deer each to each bleat;
食野之蒿。	Afield south'rnwood they eat.
我有嘉宾，	I have good guests today;
德音孔昭。	Good virtues they display.
视民不恌，	They teach folks not to steal,
君子是则是效。	The lord's their ideal and weal.
我有旨酒，	I have good food and wine;
嘉宾式燕以敖。	Happily, happily my guests dine.
呦呦鹿鸣，	The deer each to each bleat;
食野之芩。	Afield scullcaps they eat.
我有嘉宾，	I have good guests today;
鼓瑟鼓琴。	The lute and lyre we play.
鼓瑟鼓琴，	The lute and lyre we play;
和乐且湛。	We are so happy and gay.
我有旨酒，	I have good food and wine.
以燕乐嘉宾之心。	Merrily, merrily my guests dine.

11. 常棣　Cherry Blossoms

常棣之华，	Cherry blossoms blow finc;
鄂不韡韡。	Even the sepals shine.
凡今之人，	No one, one or other
莫如兄弟。	Is like a real brother.
死丧之威，	When faced with threat or scare
兄弟孔怀。	Brothers mutually care.
原隰裒矣，	On low land they gather
兄弟永矣。	And help out each other.
脊令在原，	In need a wagtail's made;
兄弟急难。	His brothers run to his aid.
每有良朋，	Good friends only stand by.
况也求叹。	Seek their help?You but sigh.
兄弟阋于墙，	Brothers fight at home though;
外御其务。	Outside they fight their foe.
每有良朋，	Oftentimes a good friend
烝也无戎。	Does not a hand extend.
丧乱既平，	When over is the strife,
既安且宁。	They lead a peaceful life.
虽有兄弟，	At this time brotherhood
不如友生。	Cannot match friendship good.
傧尔笾豆，	The bowls are placed in line;
饮酒之饫。	The brothers drink good wine.

兄弟既具，	Today siblings unite
和乐且孺。	In concord and delight.
妻子好合，	Children and wife are boon
如鼓琴瑟。	Like lute and flute in tune.
兄弟既翕，	Today brothers unite
和乐且湛。	In concert and delight.
宜尔室家，	In your family dear
乐尔妻帑。	Make children and wife cheer.
是究是图，	Practice in word and deed,
亶其然乎。	And a good life you'll lead.

12. 采薇 Vetch We Pick

采薇采薇，	Vetch we pick, vetch we pick;
薇亦作止。	The vetch sprouting so quick.
曰归曰归，	Home we wend, home we wend;
岁亦莫止。	The year comes to an end.
靡室靡家，	We have no home to go,
猃狁之故。	Due to the Huns, our foe.
不遑启居，	We have no time to rest;
猃狁之故。	The Huns do us molest.
采薇采薇，	Vetch we pick, vetch we pick,
薇亦柔止。	The vetch slender and thick.
曰归曰归，	Home we wend, home we wend;
心亦忧止。	Our hearts are bound to rend.
忧心烈烈，	Our hearts going to burst,

载饥载渴。	We bear hunger and thirst.
我戍未定，	The war remains on fire;
靡使归聘。	Who'll go home to inquire?
采薇采薇，	Vetch we pick, vetch we pick,
薇亦刚止。	The vetch stalk like a stick.
曰归曰归，	Home we wend, home we wend;
岁亦阳止。	New Year will now spring send.
王事靡盬，	The war's meeting a seethe;
不遑启处。	We have no time to breathe.
忧心孔疚，	Our hearts laden with care,
我行不来！	Go back home we can ne'er.
彼尔维何？	What's the bloom facing thee?
维常之华。	A bloom of cherry tree.
彼路斯何？	Lo, chariot. What a thing!
君子之车。	The chariot of our king.
戎车既驾，	The chariot rolls along;
四牡业业。	The four steeds look so strong.
岂敢定居？	How dare we lay down arms?
一月三捷。	One month we've three alarms.
驾彼四牡，	His guards the chariot drive;
四牡骙骙。	The four steeds gallop live.
君子所依，	The king afore does ride;
小人所腓。	Behind we soldiers hide.
四牡翼翼，	The steeds charge in a row;
象弭鱼服。	There shine arrow and bow.

岂不日戒？
玁狁孔棘！

We'd always stand on guard;
The Huns press us so hard.

昔我往矣，
杨柳依依。
今我来思，
雨雪霏霏。
行道迟迟，
载渴载饥。
我心伤悲，
莫知我哀！

When we left long ago,
The willows waved adieu.
Now back to our hometown,
We meet snow falling down.
The way gets worse and worst;
We bear hunger and thirst.
O our hearts full of woe,
Who does our sorrow know?

第二节 《楚辞》
Section 2 *Ch'u Verse*

1. 离骚（节选） Woebegone (excerpt)

帝高阳之苗裔兮，
朕皇考曰伯庸。

O I'm a descendant from Lord High Sun[①];
And my late father was called Use One[②].

---

① Lord High Sun: Plump Head, Chuan Hsiu if transliterated, Lord Yellow's grandson, named after the capital of his fief, High Sun, in today's Ch'i County, Honan Province.

② Use One: Poyung if transliterated, the author's father. "Use" in the name is a code of an important philosophical concept of doing, performance, practice or utility in contrast with the ultimate ontological "Word" or "Being" while "One" indicates his primogeniture as the first son.

摄提贞于孟陬兮，

惟庚寅吾以降。

O in Prime Spring[①], Jupiter[②] came to shine

O'er my birth on Tiger[③], a month fine.

皇览揆余初度兮，

肇锡余以嘉名。

O my sire observed the hour when came I

And gave me auspicious names thereby.

名余曰正则兮，

字余曰灵均。

O my formal address was Rule Right[④],

And my familiar one was Fair Sprite[⑤].

纷吾既有此内美兮，

又重之以修能。

O with inner beauty I was so well blessed,

And to raise my own worth I tried best.

扈江离与辟芷兮，

纫秋兰以为佩。

---

① Prime Spring: the first moon according to Chinese calendar.

② Jupiter: the yearly star in Chinese astrology and astronomy, the fifth planet from the sun, around which it revolves about 12 (117/8) years at a mean distance of 483,000,000 miles. And Jupiter is a year because its orbit, close to the ecliptic, is divided into twelve parts, which represent 12 years, and accordingly one year is called one Jupiter year, Jupiter for short.

③ Tiger: name of a lunar month, approximately the period between Beginning of Spring and Stunned.

④ Rule Right: the formal address of our poet, Yüan Ch'ü (cir. 340 B.C. －cir. 278 B.C.). According to *The Rites of Chough*, a boy is given his formal name three months after his birth, used on formal or ceremonial occasions.

⑤ Fair Sprite: our poet's familiar address. In ancient China, a boy was given his familiar name when he had grown up to manhood at the age of twenty, addressed by his relatives and friends for daily use.

O selinea[①]'n angelica[②] I don;

A eupatory[③] sash I put on.

汩余若将不及兮，

恐年岁之不吾与。

O the tide I can't catch up with runs fast;

The time that does not wait for me flies past!

朝搴阰之木兰兮，

夕揽洲之宿莽。

O at dawn on slope magnolias[④] I amass;

At eve at shoal I pick lodging-grass[⑤].

日月忽其不淹兮，

春与秋其代序。

O Sun and Moon, for e'er you turn and speed;

Spring and autumn each other succeed.

惟草木之零落兮，

恐美人之迟暮。

O there appear withering trees and grass;

I fear the beauty may fade, alas.

长太息以掩涕兮，

哀民生之多艰。

---

① selinea: an aromatic herb, an umbelliferous plant one to two feet tall, often knit into apparels or braided as pendants.

② angelica: an odoriferous herb over four feet tall, blowing small white flowers in clusters in summer, usually used as a decoration for sashes or pendants in ancient China. Its roots often candied as a confection.

③ eupatory: an aromatic herb, growing by waterside, with purple stems, red at protuberant joints, four to five feet tall, with glossy leaves which are long, pointed at end and saw-toothed on edges, luxuriant in summer.

④ magnolia: any of a genus (*Magnolia*) of trees or shrubs with barks like those of the cinnamon and with large, fragrant and usually showy flowers.

⑤ lodging-grass: a perennial aromatic grass extinct now, a coined term based on the motivation of Chinese Sumang (su: lodging; mang: grass) said to be able to stand having its heart plucked away without dying, a symbol of fidelity, goodness and permanence.

O with a long sigh, I wipe away my tears;

How hard the folk's life is, months and years!

余虽好修姱以鞿羁兮，

謇朝谇而夕替。

O although I'm self-disciplined, trying to be chaste,

At morn I counsel, at eve debased.

既替余以蕙纕兮，

又申之以揽茝。

O they curse me for the basil I wear

And then for my angelica fair.

亦余心之所善兮，

虽九死其犹未悔。

O to remain worthy and pure I try;

I won't regret e'en if nine times I'll die.

路曼曼其修远兮，

吾将上下而求索。

O the roadway rolls on to twist and turn;

I'll seek and search, up and down I yearn.

2. 少司命（节选） Life God Junior[①] (excerpt)

秋兰兮麋芜，

罗生兮堂下。

Orchid[②], lovage[③], o aligned,

Grow neath the hall, o you find.

---

① Life God Junior: God in charge of the reproduction of people's posterity.

② orchid: any of a widely distributed family of terrestrial or epiphytic monocotyledonous plants having thickened bulbous roots and often very showy distinctive flowers.

③ lovage: a selinea-like herb, cultivated as a sweet herb, and for the use in herbal medicine of its root, and to a less degree, the leaves and seeds.

3. 惜往日（节选）Missing the Bygone Day (excerpt)

芳与泽其杂糅兮，
孰申旦而别之？
O fragrance and luster can blend so well;
Who can the difference so clearly tell.

背法度而心治兮，
辟与此其无异。
O you do not rule with law but your mind,
As clear as the similes you may find.

4. 橘颂 Ode to the Orange

后皇嘉树，
橘徕服兮。
King of trees, of the best,
O accustomed, you're grand.
受命不迁，
生南国兮。
Now settled, never moved,
O you grow in South Land.
深固难徙，
更壹志兮。
Deeply rooted, so staid,
O you're focused and willed.
绿叶素荣，
纷其可喜兮。
With leaves green and flowers white,
O with such glee you're fulfilled.

曾枝剡棘，
圆果抟兮。
Leaf upon leaf, with thorns,
O you've fruit round and fine.
青黄杂糅，
文章烂兮。
With yellow out of green,
O you have hues to shine.
精色内白，
类可任兮。
With pure skin, a white heart,
O you're out of the Way.
纷缊宜修，
姱而不丑兮。
So fragrant and so spruce,
O not plain, grace you display.
嗟尔幼志，
有以异兮。
How great, a great young will!
O unique you're to me!
独立不迁，
岂不可喜兮?
Independent, unchanged,
O isn't your state our glee?
深固难徙，
廓其无求兮。
So settled, moved no more,
O broad-minded, you stand tall.
苏世独立，

横而不流兮。
Straightforward and detached,
O to the dust you don't fall.
闭心自慎，
不终失过兮。
Circumspect and discreet,
O you've never gone awry.
秉德无私，
参天地兮。
Unselfish and virtuous,
You tower twixt earth and sky.
愿岁并谢，
与长友兮。
With you I would share all,
O be good friends for long.
淑离不淫，
梗其有理兮。
Graceful and not obscene,
O you're rational and strong.
年岁虽少，
可师长兮。
Although you are so young,
You're my teacher, my bro.
行比伯夷，
置以为像兮。
You are well placed in here,
O my icon like Great Bow①.

① Great Bow: Bow One, so named because of being firstborn. There are two notables known by the name Great Bow or Bow One in Chinese history. The first one is the grand priest in Lord Mound's time, in charge of rites and criminal law; the second is the elder prince of the lord of Lonebamboo, a vassal state of Shang, who died of starvation at Mt. Firstshine to maintain his rectitude.

5. 天问（节选）Asking the Sky (excerpt)

曰：遂古之初，
谁传道之？
I'd ask: When Beginning began,
Who made it, by which man?
上下未形，
何由考之？
Not formed, Heaven and earth;
Who's it that gave them birth?
冥昭瞢暗，
谁能极之？
Chaos, so blurred and dim,
Who can reach to the brim?
冯翼惟象，
何以识之？
This icon does there rise;
This who can recognize?
明明暗暗，
惟时何为？
Shine in shine, shade in shade,
When was it like this made?
阴阳三合，
何本何化？
Shine and Shade and Man too,
What's the root, fruit, or cue?
圜则九重，
孰营度之？
The dome has nine folds, true!

Who has measured it, who?
惟兹何功，
孰初作之？
What a project, how grand!
Who built it as well planned?
斡维焉系，
天极焉加？
The axis of earth, oh, where?
Where's the pole? You know e'er?
八柱何当，
东南何亏？
Where do Eight Pillars[①] face,
Southeast a sunken place?
九天之际，
安放安属？
Within the nine broad skies,
Where are their links and ties?
隅隈多有，
谁知其数？
Corners, edges, all those,
Who knows the count, who knows?
天何所沓？
十二焉分？
Where do Sky and Earth meet?
Why twelve parts so discreet?
日月安属？

① Eight Pillars: the eight pillars propping up the sky in Chinese mythology, also a metaphor for the mainstay of a cause.

列星安陈?

How suns and moons align?

How are stars placed to shine?

出自汤谷，

次于蒙汜。

Suns rise from Sunrise Dell①

And in Haze Flow② they dwell.

6. 渔父 The Fisherman

屈原既放，游于江潭，行吟泽畔，颜色憔悴，形容枯槁。渔父见而问之曰："子非三闾大夫与？何故至于斯？"

Yüan Ch'ü③, now exiled, wanders along the river, roving and chanting onto the marsh, so haggard and skinny. A fisherman, seeing him, asks: "Aren't you Lord of Three Portals④, why reduced to such a state?"

屈原曰：

"举世皆浊我独清，

众人皆醉我独醒，

是以见放。"

Yüan Ch'ü replies:

"I'm exiled because

① Sunrise Dell: the place where the ten suns rise according to Chinese mythology.

② Haze Flow: the place where the ten suns set for the night according to Chinese mythology.

③ Yüan Ch'ü: cir. 340 B.C.—cir. 278 B.C., our poet, a loyal minister of Ch'u and a great patriot of China, who threw himself into the River Milo, wronged by his king and other aristocrats and so aggrieved at his broken land. He is esteemed as father of Chinese poetry by virtue of being the first named poet of importance and the author of the great and exceptionally long poem Woebegone. He is well-liked in China and East Asia. May Fifth of each year, known as the Dragon Boat Festival, is the day when all Chinese and many East Asians like Koreans, Japanese, Vietnamese, Burmese, Malays and so on celebrate this poet, one of the greatest poets of all time.

④ Lord of Three Portals: the title of a minister who holds a special position instituted in the State of Ch'u, mainly in charge of sacrificial rituals and education of the young of the three noble families of Ch'u, i.e. Chao, Ch'ü and Ching.

All the world but me is sunken;
All the crowd but me is drunken."
渔父曰：
"圣人不凝滞于物，
而能与世推移。
世人皆浊，
何不淈其泥而扬其波？
众人皆醉，
何不餔其糟而歠其釃？
何故深思高举，
自令放为？"
The fisherman says:
"A saint is not stuck but changing with the world.
Since the world is sunken,
Why not roil the mud and splash the blue?
Since the crowd is drunken,
Why not eat the draff and drink the brew?
Why so profound and high flown that you've got exiled?"
屈原曰："吾闻之：
新沐者必弹冠，
新浴者必振衣。
安能以身之察察，
受物之汶汶者乎？
宁赴湘流，
葬于江鱼之腹中。
安能以皓皓之白，
而蒙世俗之尘埃乎？"
Yüan Ch'ü replies: "I hear:

He who's newly bathed must pat his crown;

He who's newly washed must shakc his gown.

Clean and clean I remain;

How can I myself stain?

I'd rather go to the Hsiang① stream

And be eaten up by a bream②.

I should keep chaste and pure, and I must;

How can I drift and breathe the dust?"

渔父莞尔而笑，鼓枻而去。

歌曰：

The old fisherman shows a thin smile and leaves, plying his oar while chanting:

"沧浪之水清兮，

可以濯吾缨；

沧浪之水浊兮，

可以濯吾足。"

"The Blue③'s stream is limpid,

Wherewith I wash my sash;

The Blue's stream is turbid,

Wherewith I wash my feet."

遂去，不复与言。

Thus leaves he, speaking no more.

---

① the Hsiang: the Hsiang River, the biggest river in today's Hunan Province, a branch of the Long River, a major source of Lake Cavehall.

② bream: a fresh water cyprinoid fish.

③ the Blue: the Blue River, which might be the Han River or its branch or the Summer River.

第三节 《文心雕龙》

Section 3 *Carve the Dragon with Your Literary Heart*

1. 原道 Back to the Word

文之为德也大矣，与天地并生者，何哉？夫玄黄色杂，方圆体分，日月叠璧，以垂丽天之象；山川焕绮，以铺理地之形：此盖道之文也。仰观吐曜，俯察含章，高卑定位，故两仪既生矣。惟人参之，性灵所钟，是谓三才。为五行之秀气，实天地之心生。心生而言立，言立而文明，自然之道也。旁及万品，动植皆文。龙凤以藻绘呈瑞，虎豹以炳蔚凝姿；云霞雕色，有逾画工之妙；草木贲华，无待锦匠之奇。夫岂外饰，盖自然耳。至于林籁结响，调如竽瑟；泉石激韵，和若球锽。故形立则章成矣，声发则文生矣。夫以无识之物，郁然有彩，有心之器，其无文欤？

Great is the virtue of literature! It began with Heaven and earth. Why? With the emergence of Heaven and earth was the division of yellow and dark, and of square and round. Suns and moons like layered jade revealed the icons in Heaven, hills and rills like brilliant brocade showed the layout and texture of earth. This is the literature of the Word. High above, suns and moons give off sparkles; down below, hills and rills roll with splendor. With the determination of Heaven being high and earth being low, Two Wings came into being. Humans joined them, fully spirited, hence Three Gifts[①]. Humans are souls of all things, actually the mind of Heaven and earth. The mind gives rise to language, and language to civilization, as is the course of nature. As is extended to all things, flora and fauna are literate: dragons and phoenixes are blessed with colored hues; tigers and leopards are painted with brilliant stripes. Clouds in the sky outshine the exquisite designs by artists; flowers of grass and plants decline the gifts of craftsmen. Have they been beautified? No, they are natural. Hark, a sough

---

① Three Gifts: referring to Heaven, Earth and Man.

through the woods is like a flute melody, and the gurgle upon the pebbles is a lute harmony. So, form established, sound activated, literature comes to be. Even senseless natural things are rich with literature. Aren't intelligent men literate?

第四节　李白诗歌
Section 4　Pai Li's Poems

1. 静夜思 Night Thought

床前看月光，
疑是地上霜。
举头望山月，
低头思故乡。

The moon[1] sheds light before the bed[2],
Which seems to be frost on the ground.
To the bright moon, I raise my head,
And lower it to muse, for home bound.

① the moon: the satellite of the earth, an important image in Chinese literature or culture as it can evoke many associations such as solitude and nostalgia on the one hand, and purity, brightness and happy reunions on the other. In traditional times, there used to be a "moon-viewing party," at which people sat quietly on a moonlit night, particularly under a full moon, and thought of a loved one or loved ones far away, inside the vast reaches of China proper and even overseas, who might themselves be sitting sharing the same moon at the same time, in the same reverent silence.

② the bed: probably a flower bed in a yard, because looking at the moon in a room seems to be improbable.

2. 清平调（其一）Pure Peace Tune, No.1[①]

云想衣裳花想容，
春风拂槛露华浓。
若非群玉山头见，
会向瑶台月下逢。

Her dress like plumage and her face a rose,
Breeze pets the rails and the belle in repose.
If not a fairy queen from Heav'n on high,
She's Goddess of Moon that makes rosebuds shy.

3. 峨眉山月歌 A Song of the Moon o'er Mt. Brow

峨眉山月半轮秋，
影入平羌江水流。
夜发清溪向三峡，
思君不见下渝州。

Half a disc of moon over Mt. Brow[②] glows;
Its autumn shadow cast to the Peace flows[③].
From Clear Creek to Three Gorges[④] I go at night,
Rowing past Yüchow[⑤] without you in sight.

---

① Pure Peace Tune, No.1: Pai Li's poem composed impromptu at a royal party held by Emperor Deepsire with Lady Yang in the Pavilion of Aloes on a spring day. The tree-peonies newly imported from India were in full bloom as if in rivalry of beauty with the emperor's voluptuous mistress. There were the musicians of the Pear Garden and the wine of grapes from Coolton. Pai Li was summoned, because his art could capture for eternity the glory of the vanishing hours.

② Mt. Brow: Mt. Omei if transliterated, a famous mountain located in Shu.

③ the Peace flows: Pingch'iang if transliterated, a river located in Shu.

④ Three Gorges: referring to the three gorges of the Long River, including Big Pond Gorge, Witch Gorge, and Westridge Gorge, a set of spectacular gorges formed where the Long River cuts its way through the formi dable Witch Mountains, forming a three- hundred-kilometer stretch of very narrow canyons.

⑤ Yüchow: a former name of Ch'ungch'ing.

4. 黄鹤楼送孟浩然之广陵 Seeing off Haojan Meng① to Broadridge② at Yellow Crane Tower

故人西辞黄鹤楼，
烟花三月下扬州。
孤帆远影碧山尽，
唯见长江天际流。

Yellow Crane③ to my old friend now says bye;
Amid March catkins④, to Yangchow⑤ he'll go.
The lonely sail fades to merge with the mountain;
Lo, beside Heavens the Yangtze does flow.

5. 宣州谢朓楼饯别校书叔云 Seeing Off Yün, My Uncle, a Collator, on T'iao Hsieh⑥'s Tower in Hsuan⑦

弃我去者，昨日之日不可留；
乱我心者，今日之日多烦忧。
长风万里送秋雁，

---

① Haojan Meng: Haojan Meng (A.D. 689 – A.D. 740), a renowned pastoral poet, Pai Li's good friend, ranking next to Pai Li and Fu Tu in the entire galaxy of the poets of the glorious T'ang Empire, but unfulfilled officially, he lived in reclusion almost all his life.

② Broadridge: an alternative name for Yangchow, a land of Wu in the Spring and Autumn period, belonging to Stripfour (576 B.C. – 484 B.C.), who declined the throne and farmed in Broadridge. It became the most prosperous port city in the T'ang dynasty because of the Peking-Hangchow Canal dug by the previous dynasty and it was a waterland like today's Venice, attracting businessmen, travelers, monks and courtesans from every part of the country and the world.

③ Yellow Crane: Yellow Crane Tower, a famous tower built by Wu in A.D. 223, located on the top of Mt. Snake, overlooking the Long River, in present-day Wuhan, Hupei Province.

④ catkin: a deciduous scaly spike of flowers, as in the willow, an image of helpless drifting or wandering in Chinese literature.

⑤ Yangchow: alias Broadridge, an important city in today's Chiangsu Province, the greatest port in China and the centre of luxury trades in the T'ang dynasty.

⑥ T'iao Hsieh: T'iao Hsieh (A.D. 464 – A.D. 499), an outstanding highborn landscape poet. He was appointed prefecture of Hsuan in A.D. 495 and then director of the Board of Civil Affairs, and died in prison due to a false charge.

⑦ Hsuan: an ancient town or prefecture in present-day Hsuan, Anhui Province.

对此可以酣高楼。
蓬莱文章建安骨，
中间小谢又清发。
俱怀逸兴壮思飞，
欲上青天览明月。
抽刀断水水更流，
举杯消愁愁更愁。
人生在世不称意，
明朝散发弄扁舟。

What deserts me is yesterday that has gone away;
What disturbs me is today that does me dismay.
The wind blows a thousand miles for wild geese①;
Let's go upstairs, let's drink to the spry breeze.
Your verses are pithy with colors clean②;
My poems are pretty like branches green.
Full of pride, so elegant, we would fly
To pick up the shining moon from the sky.
Cut off the flow, and we will see more flow;
Drink off our woe, and we will have more woe.
Life is hard, such a harassing affair;
Let's row tomorrow, disheveled our hair.

6. 长相思 Long Longing

长相思，在长安。
络纬秋啼金井阑，

---

① wild goose: an undomesticated goose that is caring and responsible, taken as a symbol of benevolence, righteousness, good manner, wisdom, and faith in Chinese culture.

② Your verses are pithy with colors clean: referring to the style of Making Peace, i.e., the third reign title of Emperor Hsien (A.D. 181－A.D. 234) of the Eastern Han, when literature flourished.

微霜凄凄簟色寒。
孤灯不明思欲绝，
卷帷望月空长叹。
美人如花隔云端，
上有青冥之高天，
下有渌水之波澜。
天长路远魂飞苦，
梦魂不到关山难。
长相思，摧心肝。
My longing stretches to the capital.
Neath the rails cheep crickets ephemeral;
My mat feels cold as frost begins to fall.
The lone lamp dims and my sad tears run dry;
Rolling up the curtain, to the moon I sigh.
The belle looms like a rosebud in the sky.
High above extends the infinite blue;
Down below a tumult of waves do flow.
Time hangs on my hand and the way's far-flung;
The mountain passes cannot hear my song.
My longing, rending my heart, stretches long.

7. 赠汪伦 To Lun Wang

李白乘舟将欲行，
忽闻岸上踏歌声。
桃花潭水深千尺，
不及汪伦送我情。
While I'm leaving now to the boat embark,
A song from the bank treads in with beats, hark.

A thousand feet deep is the Peach Bloom Pond[①],
But not deeper than my friend's love so fond.

8. 上李邕 To Yung Li[②]

大鹏一日同风起，
抟摇直上九万里。
假令风歇时下来，
犹能簸却沧溟水。
时人见我恒殊调，
闻余大言皆冷笑。
宣父犹能畏后生，
丈夫未可轻年少。

One day the roc[③] with the wind does arise
Ninety thousand miles up to the blue skies.
If the wind slows down and inclines to stop,
It'll turn the sea upside down with a flop.
The world may regard my talk as so queer;
Hearing me like that, at my words they jeer.
Teacher[④] said a child may strike one with awe;
One should never a little child ignore!

---

① the Peach Bloom Pond: a pond in Ching County under the jurisdiction of Hsuan, with a bucolic scene of Peach Blossom Source depicted by Lord Glee, that is, Lingyün Hsieh (A.D.385 – A.D.433). Here, a villager called Lun Wang treated Pai Li with wine and saw him off with the simplicity of true love. Lun's descendants cherish this poem till now.

② Yung Li: A.D.678 – A.D. 747, a famous poet and calligrapher, and an outspoken official, killed later by Premier Linfu Li out of schemes and intrigues.

③ roc: in Arabian and Persian legend, an enormous and powerful bird of prey. According to Sir Lush, the giant bird is a symbol of universal force or the operation of such a force, as reads like this: There in North Sea is a fish called Minnow, whose body spans about a thousand miles. When transformed into a bird, it is called Roc, whose back spans about a thousand miles.

④ Teacher: referring to Confucius, who had 72 outstanding disciples out of several thousand students, extolled as a teacher of all by emperors, scholars and the general population in later generations.

9. 将进酒 Do Drink Wine[①]

君不见黄河之水天上来，
奔流到海不复回。
君不见高堂明镜悲白发，
朝如青丝暮成雪。
人生得意须尽欢，
莫使金樽空对月。

Don't you espy
The Yellow River[②] surge down from the sky,
Up to the sea it does tumble and flow?
Don't you espy
To my white hair in the mirror I sigh,
As at dawn is black and at dusk turns snow?
Do enjoy life while in prime you run high;
Not to the moon just your empty cup ply.

天生我材必有用，
千金散尽还复来。
烹羊宰牛且为乐，
会须一饮三百杯。

So born by Heaven[③] we must be of use;
Spend all the money and more will come up.

---

① wine: Drinking plays an important part in the lives of most Chinese, especially Chinese poets, acting as a form of enlightenment comparable to zen practice. Wine is a must at a feast, as is said, without wine, there will be no feast.

② the Yellow River: the second longest river in China, flowing through Loess Plateau, hence yellow water all the way, 5,464 kilometers long, with a drainage area of 752,443 square kilometers. It has been regarded as the cradle of Chinese civilization. As legend goes, the river derived from a yellow dragon that, couchant on Midland Plain, ate yellow soil, flooded crops, devoured people and stock, and was finally tamed by Great Worm, the First King of Hsia (cir. 2070 B.C.－1600 B.C.).

③ Heaven: the space surrounding or seeming to overarch the earth, in which the sun, the moon, and stars appear, popularly the abode of God, his angels and the blessed, and in most cases suggesting supernatural power or sometimes signifying a monarch.

Cook lamb, kill cattle just for joy profuse;

Do gulp down three hundred fills from your cup.

岑夫子，

丹丘生，

将进酒，

杯莫停。

与君歌一曲，

请君为我倾耳听。

Ts'en, my teacher,

Redknoll[①], friend mine,

Don't put down cups,

Do drink the wine.

I'll sing you a song of cheer,

Please listen, prick up your ear.

钟鼓馔玉不足贵，

但愿长醉不用醒。

古来圣贤皆寂寞，

惟有饮者留其名。

Bells, drums and dainties are precious no more;

Drink ourselves drunk, ne'er sober, lying down.

Obscure are the sages and saints of yore,

Only drinkers can enjoy high renown.

陈王昔时宴平乐，

斗酒十千恣欢谑。

主人何为言少钱，

径须沽取对君酌。

① Ts'en and Redknoll: Pai Li's Wordist friends.

At olden times Prince Ch'en[①] held a great feast;
He drank barrels and barrels with no stall.
How can a host claim to have money least?
I shall buy more and drink up to you all.
五花马，
千金裘，
呼儿将出换美酒，
与尔同销万古愁。
Dapples[②] be sold,
And furs like gold.
Call our son to pawn them, buy wine, buy more,
With you I will drink off our age-long sore.

10. 蜀道难 The Shu Way Is Hard

噫吁戏，危乎高哉！
蜀道之难，难于上青天。
蚕丛及鱼凫，
开国何茫然。
尔来四万八千岁，
不与秦塞通人烟。
西当太白有鸟道，
可以横绝峨眉巅。
地崩山摧壮士死，
然后天梯石栈相钩连。
上有六龙回日之高标，

---

① Prince Ch'en: referring to Chih Ts'ao (A.D. 192 – A.D. 232), the third son of the overlord Ts'ao Ts'ao. So talented and dissolute, he failed to ascend the throne but succeeded as a poet, remembered as a representative of Making Peace Literature in Chinese history.
② dapple: an animal whose skin or fur is spotted, a horse in this poem.

下有冲波逆折之回川。
黄鹤之飞尚不得过，
猿猱欲度愁攀援。
青泥何盘盘，
百步九折萦岩峦。
扪参历井仰胁息，
以手抚膺坐长叹。
问君西游何时还？
畏途巉岩不可攀。
但见悲鸟号古木，
雄飞雌从绕林间。
又闻子规啼夜月，愁空山。
蜀道之难，难于上青天，
使人听此凋朱颜。
连峰去天不盈尺，
枯松倒挂倚绝壁。
飞湍瀑流争喧豗，
砯崖转石万壑雷。
其险也若此，
嗟尔远道之人胡为乎来哉！
剑阁峥嵘而崔嵬，
一夫当关，万夫莫开。
所守或匪亲，化为狼与豺。
朝避猛虎，
夕避长蛇，
磨牙吮血，
杀人如麻。
锦城虽云乐，
不如早还家。

蜀道之难，难于上青天，
侧身西望长咨嗟。

Oh, wow, my! What a height, so high!
The Shu① way is so hard, harder than climbing the sky!
When did Silkworm② and Fishduck③
Begin their realm? It's hard to say.
Since then it's been forty eight thousand years;
Between here and Ch'in Land there is no way.
Mt. Venus④ in the west birds can fly o'er;
On to the top of Mt. Brow⑤ flap they may.
The earth sunk, mountains crushed, the brave men died⑥,
Hence the sky ladder and stack path relay.
Up, the peak barring Apollo's cart⑦ by six dragons⑧ drawn;
Down, the waves swirling and surging up to the Milky Way⑨.
Yellow cranes flying there at the height cringe;
Chimpanzees would climb but to start they sway.

---

① Shu: one of the earliest kingdoms in China, founded by Silkworm according to legend.

② Silkworm: the founder of the Kingdom of Shu, who taught his people how to raise silkworms, hence regarded as God of Silkworm-breeding.

③ Fishduck: one of the earliest kings of Shu, regarded as Gods of Fishing.

④ Mt. Venus: the highest peak of Ch'in Ridge, a Wordist sanctuary, known for its height, coldness, dangerousness, strangeness and bountifulness.

⑤ Mt. Brow: one of the four Buddhist mountains, located in Ssuch'uan Province, named for its elegant brow-shaped silhouette viewed from a distance.

⑥ The earth sunk...: According to legend, King of Shu sent five strong men to pick up the five belles given by King Hui of Ch'in. On their way back, they saw a serpent sneak into a cave. A brave man seized its tail, and the other four pulled it out with all their strength. In an instant, the earth sank and the mountain crushed and buried the men and the belles. Thus, the mountain cracked into five peaks, which made a way to Shu.

⑦ Apollo's cart: As legend goes, Apollo or God of Sun (a Goddess named Good Air, actually) rode a cart pulled by six dragons across the sky everyday.

⑧ dragon: Though variously understood as a large reptile, a marine monster, a jackal and Satan incarnate, it is also a kind protector in folklore and myth in Western culture, a mascot on the national flag of Wales. And in the East, it has been represented as a fabulous serpent-like giant winged animal that can change its length and girth, a totem of the Chinese nation and a symbol of benevolence and sovereignty in Chinese culture.

⑨ the Milky Way: the Silver River in Chinese mythology, a luminous band circling the heavens composed of stars and nebulae; the Galaxy.

The Clay Ridge[①] circles up,
Bending and twisting around the rocks gray.
From star to star you hold your breath to feel,
And palming your chest, you sit down to sigh.
Now going west, when will you come back then?
It's dangerous to climb the crags so high.
Behold, the birds wail over olden trees,
Male leading female, round the wood they fly.
Hark, on the barren hill, the cuckoos to the moon cry[②].
The Shu way is so hard, harder than climbing the sky;
At this you are too scared to run your eye.
The range is less than a foot from the blue;
Rotten pines hang upside down in cliffs high.
Water dashes rocks and turns like thunder;
Waterfalls and whirlpools noisily vie.
It's so dangerous!
Why have you come here all the way from afar, why?
Sword Pavilion[③] towering juts steeply up;
If one man holds the pass, all invaders will die.
Those stationed are kindred and kin,
Otherwise, they'd rebel like wolves sly.
At dusk snakes you evade;
At dawn tigers you shun;
A snake may bite for fun;

① the Clay Ridge: located on the border of present-day Kansu and Sha'anhsi provinces. There are rainy cliffs precipitous enough to block the passage by clay.

② the cuckoos to the moon cry: It is said that during the Shang dynasty, Cuckoo (Yü Tu), a caring king of Shu, abdicated the throne due to a flood and lived in reclusion. After his death, he became a cuckoo, wailing day and night, shedding tears and blood.

③ Sword Pavilion: a strategic pass with a plank road built along cliffs in modern-day Ssuch'uan Province.

A tiger may bloody run.

Tho Silkton① is such a good place,

You'd better go back home anon.

The Shu way is so hard, harder than climbing the sky!

Turning west to gaze, hopelessly you sigh.

第五节　杜甫诗歌
Section 5　Fu Tu's Poems

1. 春望 A View of Spring

国破山河在，

城春草木深。

感时花溅泪，

恨别鸟惊心。

烽火连三月，

家书抵万金。

白头搔更短，

浑欲不胜簪。

The state broken, the land we keep;

The spring grass in the town grows deep.

Touched by hard times②, blossoms shed tears;

Dispersed by war, birds cringe in fears.

For months the beacon③ fires have run;

---

① Silkton: the other name of Ch'engtu for it was a town of silk.

② hard times: referring to Lushan An's Rebellion. In the eleventh moon of A.D. 755, Lushan An turned traitor and captured cities and forts in a few months, forcing the emperor to flee to Ssuch'uan.

③ beacon: a prominent building set on a wall or hill or a similar position, as a guide or warning to garrison generals or others.

News from home's warmer than the sun.
Scratching my head, I feel hair thin,
Which could not hold up my hat pin.

2. 赠花卿 To Hua[①], a General

锦城丝管日纷纷，
半入江风半入云。
此曲只应天上有，
人间能得几回闻？
In Silkton there the tune of flutes or strings
Half to a river wind, half to clouds rings.
Such music should be a Heavenly tune;
One can only hear once in a blue moon.

3. 月夜忆舍弟 Missing My Brothers[②] on a Moonlit Night

戍鼓断人行，
边秋一雁声。
露从今夜白，
月是故乡明。
有弟皆分散，
无家问死生。
寄书长不达，
况乃未休兵。
Watch drum[③] on and off, traffics cease;
The border hears shrills of wild geese.

---

① Hua: General Hua under Kuangyin Ts'ui, Mayor of Ch'engtu.
② my brothers: Fu Tu had four brothers, Ying Tu, Kuan Tu, Feng Tu and Chan Tu.
③ watch drum: a drum on a watch tower.

Autumn dew turns frost from tonight①;
My town should see the moon so bright.
My brothers were driven asunder;
"Are they alive or dead?" I wonder.
It's long for news to come to hand,
And now the war fire sears my land.

4. 旅夜书怀 Traveling at Night

细草微风岸，
危樯独夜舟。
星垂平野阔，
月涌大江流。
名岂文章著，
官应老病休。
飘飘何所似，
天地一沙鸥。
Thin grass ashore stirs with a blast;
My boat sails at night, a high mast.
The stars hang low o'er the broad plain;
The moonlit river pours amain.
One's not famed from a writing quill;
He should retire when old and ill.
Drifting, drifting, where shall I lie,
A seagull② between sea and sky?

---

① Autumn dew turns frost from tonight: referring to White Dew, the fifteenth of the twenty-four terms of the year.

② seagull: a kind of sea bird, any gull or large tern, a symbol of clean integrity. The seagulls in the Wordist book *Sir Line* (*Liehtzu*) are particularly sensitive to impurity of motive and will make friends only with the completely guileless and disinterested. It is also used as metaphor for drifting.

5. 客至 A Friend's Visit

舍南舍北皆春水，
但见群鸥日日来。
花径不曾缘客扫，
蓬门今始为君开。
盘飧市远无兼味，
樽酒家贫只旧醅。
肯与邻翁相对饮，
隔篱呼取尽馀杯。

The spring water north and south of my hut,
Day in day out but seagulls come to view.
I've never swept my petal-strewn path but
Today my thatched gate is opened for you.
Town off, I've no dainties to entertain;
All I have to drink is home-brewed wine.
Drink with my old neighbor if you would fain,
I'll invite him across the fence to dine.

6. 望岳 Looking at Mt. Arch

岱宗夫如何，
齐鲁青未了。
造化钟神秀，
阴阳割昏晓。
荡胸生曾云，
决眦入归鸟。
会当凌绝顶，
一览众山小。

Behold Mt. Arch[①], how high it stands!
Its green o'er Ch'i and Lu[②] expands.
The nature's made it a great one,
Shade as its moon, shine as its sun.
Unto my chest thick clouds arise;
And homing birds fly to my eyes.
When I reach the top to view all,
All mountains under me are small.

7. 春夜喜雨 A Blessing Rain on a Spring Night

好雨知时节，
当春乃发生。
随风潜入夜，
润物细无声。
野径云俱黑，
江船火独明。
晓看红湿处，
花重锦官城。

A good rain knows its time to come,
And brings things to life right in spring.
It steals into the night with wind
And mutely moistens everything.
Over wild paths, clouds are all black,

---

① Mt. Arch: one of the Five Mountains in China, located in Shantung Province, along with Mt. Ever in Shanhsi, Mt. Scale in Hunan, Mt. Flora in Sha'anhsi, and Mt. Tower in Honan. Mt. Arch is the most sacred of the five, because 72 sovereigns in prehistoric China made sacrifices to the god of the mountain and 12 emperors made sacrifices from the Ch'in dynasty to the Ch'ing dynasty, clearly recorded in history books.

② Ch'i and Lu: The north side of Mt. Arch was the ancient State of Ch'i; its south side was the State of Lu.

A boat afloat, its lone fire bright.

At daybreak one sees wet and red;

Flowers in Brocade Town[1] make a sight.

8. 饮中八仙歌 Song of Eight Drinking Immortals[2]

知章骑马似乘船，
眼花落井水底眠。
汝阳三斗始朝天，
道逢曲车口流涎，
恨不移封向酒泉。
左相日兴费万钱，
饮如长鲸吸百川，
衔杯乐圣称避贤。
宗之萧洒美少年，
举觞白眼望青天，
皎如玉树临风前。
苏晋长斋绣佛前，
醉中往往爱逃禅。
李白一斗诗百篇，
长安市上酒家眠。
天子呼来不上船，
自称臣是酒中仙。
张旭三杯草圣传，

① Brocade Town: alias Silkton, Ch'engtu, a city once prosperous with fine silk, now the capital of Ssuch'uan Province.

② Eight Drinking Immortals: The eight who are good at drinking in Long Peace are Pai Li, Chihchang Ho, Shihchih Li, Chin Li, Tsungchih Ts'ui, Chin Su, Hsu Chang, and Sui Chiao, dubbed Eight Drinking immortals. This poem consists of eight portraits of them.

脱帽露顶王公前，

挥毫落纸如云烟。

焦遂五斗方卓然，

高谈雄辨惊四筵。

Stave[①] rides his horse like sailing on a boat;

Blurred, he falls in a well and sleeps afloat.

Having drunk three pots, Shine[②] goes to court now;

Mash-cart met en route, his mouth drools enow,

Sad, he can't change his fief to Wine Spring[③], how?

Left Minister[④] gets up and spends like showers;

Like a whale he sucks in hours after hours;

Cup to his lips, he's the saint, shunning powers.

To Sire[⑤] is carefree, with handsome young eyes,

His cup raised, his pupils raised to the skies,

Gleaming like a jade tree thru soughs and sighs.

Chin[⑥] fasts before figures of Buddha men;

When he's so drunk, he tries to escape Zen.

A pot of wine drunk, Pai[⑦]'s verse may pour down;

---

① Stave: referring to Chihchang Ho, whose first name means Knowing Staves.

② Shine: referring to Chin Li, the Prince of Youshine (Juyang), Chihchang Ho's good friend.

③ Wine Spring: Spring of Wine, a city called Chiuch'üan if transliterated, in the western part of today's Kansu Province, as is said to have possessed a natural fountain of wine. According to *Myths and Marvels* (*Shen-e Ching*), in the wilderness of West China, there gurgles a fountain of wine pure like jade, more than 3 meters in width and more than 10 meters in depth and, which can revive or rejuvenate a drinker to eternal life. And a folklore source says in the Western Han dynasty, Swift Huo (140 B.C. – 117 B.C.) put his wine into the spring so that there would be an adequate supply for a celebration party after their defeating a Hun invasion, hence the name.

④ Left Minister: Shichih Li (A.D. 694 – A.D. 747), of the royal family of T'ang, prime minister, Emperor Grandsire's great grandson.

⑤ To Sire: Chungchih Ts'ui, secretary, knighted Count of Ch'i.

⑥ Chin: Chin Su (A.D. 676 – A.D. 734), from Blue Field County, a court official.

⑦ Pai: Pai Li (A.D. 701 – A.D. 762), 12 years Fu Tu's senior, a famous poet, accorded God of Wine, Fallen Immortal, and Fairy of Poetry.

He sleeps to snore in a pub of the town.

Son of Heaven calls him to go aboard;

He would not, declaring: "I am Wine Lord."

After three cups, Sunrise①, Cursive Saint, leers.

Cap dropped, head bare, he stands before the peers,

Wielding his brush, hence a great piece appears.

Only after five pots does Burn② there rise,

His eloquence does all at feast surprise.

9. 兵车行 The Chariot: A Ballad③

车辚辚，马萧萧，

行人弓箭各在腰。

耶娘妻子走相送，

尘埃不见咸阳桥。

牵衣顿足拦道哭，

哭声直上干云霄。

道旁过者问行人，

行人但云点行频。

或从十五北防河，

便至四十西营田。

---

① Sunrise: Hsu Chang, from Wu County, once Sheriff of Wu County.

② Burn: Sui Chiao, a commoner.

③ The poem makes reference to the northwestern frontiers, however, many Chinese critics believe that Fu Tu's protest was actually targeted at the disastrous campaigns in the south against the Kingdom of South Summons in 751 and after. The historical record describes popular disaffection for the South Summons campaigns in terms similar to Fu Tu's. In the northwest the loss of tens of thousands of T'ang troops in the Pyrrhic capture of the almost impregnable Stone Fortress from a few hundred Tibetans was a waste—caused by Deepsire's insistence—but it did not seriously damage the large armies operating in Central Asia. The war with the Tang's old ally South Summons was initiated through arrogant political ineptness and consummated by military ineptness as well, with the destruction of two large T'ang armies and South Summons' subsequent alliance with Tibet. Fu Tu is probably not referring to any single campaign, but to the steady drain on the peasantry caused by immoderate conscription.

去时里正与裹头，
归来头白还戍边。
边庭流血成海水，
武皇开边意未已。
君不闻，
汉家山东二百州，
千村万落生荆杞。
纵有健妇把锄犁，
禾生陇亩无东西。
况复秦兵耐苦战，
被驱不异犬与鸡。
长者虽有问，
役夫敢伸恨？
且如今年冬，
未休关西卒。
县官急索租，
租税从何出？
信知生男恶，
反是生女好。
生女犹得嫁比邻，
生男埋没随百草。
君不见，青海头，
古来白骨无人收。
新鬼烦冤旧鬼哭，
天阴雨湿声啾啾。
Chariots rattle, horses neigh;
Bow, arrows at the waist, men march their way.

Moms and dads, wives and kids rush to say bye;
Allshine Bridge[①] you can't see as dust does fly.
Pulling at clothes, stamping, blocking, they cry;
Cries rise straight up to the clouds in the sky.
A passer-by asks a man on the way:
The man replies: Troops are oft called today.
At fifteen some the River[②] north guard best;[③]
When forty they till troop farms in the west.
When they leave, Headman[④] gives them turbans mere;
Back home, hair white, then back to the frontier.
Blood on the frontier flows like an ocean,
Land extending is the Most High[⑤]'s motion.
Don't you espy
In two hundred shires east of the pass[⑥] there
All villages creep with thorns in fields bare?
Sturdy wives there are to hold hoe and plow
On lanes and slopes but they can't have enow.
E'en worse for troops in the bitterest wars,
Driven on, no different from dogs and boars.
Though you may pose the question, sir,
Does a conscript dare to demur?
And now in this winter, this year

① Allshine Bridge: on the Wei River, built in the age of Emperor Martial of Han, the indispensable route between Long Peace and the west areas.
② the River: referring to the Yellow River.
③ At fifteen some the River north guard best: young people were sent to the Yellow River to guard it well against Tibetan looters.
④ Headman: A headman, a countryside leader, manages about a hundred households in the T'ang dynasty.
⑤ the Most High: referring to Emperor Deepsire in this poem.
⑥ two hundred shires east of the pass: referring to the two hundred and seventeen prefectures east of Case Dale Pass.

They still send troops to the frontier;
County clerks demand taxes now,
But where to get taxes, and how?
To have boys is bad, as is said,
Better to have a girl instead.
Your girl to your neighbor can be married;
Your boy will be with all grasses buried.
Don't you espy by Kokonor there
Since of yore there have been white bones lay bare?
New ghosts vent their wrongs and former ghosts weep,
It's cloudy, it's raining and insects cheep.

第二章　史学
Chapter Ⅱ　History

第一节　《左传》
Section 1　*Tso's Annals*

1. 隐公十一年 The Eleventh Year Under Lord Yin

礼，经国家，定社稷，序民人，利后嗣者也。

Propriety is the way whereby to manage and defend a state, rule the people and benefit their posterity.

2. 桓公十二年 The Twelve Year Under Lord Column

公欲平宋、郑。秋，公及宋公盟于句渎之丘。宋成未可知也，故又会于虚；冬，又会于龟。宋公辞平，故与郑伯盟于武父。遂帅师而伐宋，战焉，宋无信也。君子曰："苟信不继，盟无益也。《诗》云：'君子屡盟，乱是用长。'无信也。"

Lord Column wanted to make peace with Sung and Cheng. That autumn, he formed an alliance with Lord Lush of Sung at Bent Ditch (Chütou), and later met him again at Void (Hsu) because he was not sure of Sung's sincerity In winter, they met at Turtle (Kui) and Lord Lush of Sung refused the proposal for peace. Therefore Lord Column formed alliance with Lord Sharp of Cheng at Father Martial (Wufu) and led their troops to attack Sung. The cause of the war was Sung's loss of credit. The lord said, "Without promise kept, alliance will be of no use. As *the Book of Songs* says: 'Alliances one by one, all disorders will run'. That is due to the loss of credit."

3. 庄公二十四年 The Twenty-Fourth Year of Lord Chuang

俭，德之共也；侈，恶之大也。

Frugality is a common virtue; luxury is a great sin.

4. 僖公五年 The Fifth Year Under Lord Hsi

鬼神非人实亲，惟德是依。故《周书》曰："皇天无亲，惟德是辅。"又曰："黍稷非馨，明德惟馨。"又曰："民不易物，惟德繄物。"如是，则非德，民不和，神不享矣。神所冯依，将在德矣。

Gods and ghosts are not kin, concerned with virtues only. As is stated in *Book of Chough*, "God is not biased, only assisting those who are virtuous" and "Grains are not fragrant but virtues are" and "All offer sacrifices, but God only enjoys virtuous ones. Thus, without virtue, there would be no harmony of people and God would not enjoy their sacrifice. What God cares is their virtue.

5. 僖公九年 The Ninth Year Under Lord Hsi

公家之利，知无不为，忠也；送往事居，耦俱无猜，贞也。

It is loyalty if one serves the public without reserve; it is rectitude if one respects the dead and cares for the living without doubt.

6. 僖公十三年 The Thirteenth Year Under Lord Hsi

天灾流行，国家代有，救灾恤邻，道也。

Disasters occur alternately in every state. It is the right way to relieve famine and help neighbors.

7. 僖公十四年 The Fourteenth Year Under Lord Hsi

冬，秦饥，使乞籴于晋，晋人弗与。庆郑曰："背施，无亲；幸灾，不仁；

贪爱，不祥；怒邻，不义。四德皆失，何以守国？”虢射曰：“皮之不存，毛将安傅？”庆郑曰：“弃信，背邻，患孰恤之？无信患作，失授必毙。是则然矣。”虢射曰：“无损于怨，而厚于寇，不如勿与。”庆郑曰：“背施、幸灾，民所弃也。近犹仇之，况怨敌乎？”弗听。退曰：“君其悔是哉！”

That winter, famine struck Ch'in. An envoy was sent to Chin to buy grains, but Chin refused. Ching Cheng said, “He who has no grace has no love; he who gloats is not benevolent; he who stints is unlucky; he who angers his neighbors is unjust. If the four virtues are lost, how can we defend our state?” Guo She said, “Without skin, where can hair attach to”? Ching Cheng said, “If we abandon credit and betray our neighbor, who will help us in trouble? With no credit, disasters will fall; with no rescue, our state will perish. That's the way it is.” Guo She retorted, “No decrease of Ch'in resentment but increase of their power, so we'd better not do that.” Ch'ing Cheng said, “People renounce those who abandon grace and enjoy others' misfortune. Close friends may become foes, let alone his foes.” Lord Boon of Chin did not listen. Ch'ing Cheng retired and said, “You will regret it!”

8. 文公六年 The Sixth Year of Lord Civil

宣子于是乎始为国政。制事典，正法罪，辟狱刑，董逋逃，由质要，治旧洿，本秩礼，续常职，出滞淹。既成，以授太傅阳子与太师贾佗，使行诸晋国，以为常法。

When Hsuantsu Chao reigned, he made laws, revised penal code, clarified litigation, pursued fugitives, executed deeds, stopped abuses, and restored ranks, reinstated posts and elevated talents. This having been done, he asked Grand Tutor Yangcius and Royal Instructor T'o Chia to govern the State of Chin in accordance with established laws.

9. 文公十三年 The Thirteen Year of Lord Civil

邾文公卜迁于绎。史曰："利于民而不利于君。"邾子曰："苟利于民，孤之利也。天生民而树之君，以利之也。民既利矣，孤必与焉。"左右曰："命可长也，君何弗为？"邾子曰："命在养民，死之短长，时也。民苟利矣，迁也，吉莫如之！"

Lord Civil of Chu divined the issue of moving the capital to Silk. The historiographer said: "It's good for the people but ominous for Your Lordship." The lord replied, "Anything good for the people is good for me. God created men and appointed kings for the interest of people. Anything good for people must be good for me." Officials by his side said: "All wish to live longer. Why doesn't Your Lordship?" The lord answered: "My life has been meant to raise my people and my lifespan is determined by my destiny. If moving the capital is good for people, we do it. This is the luckiest thing."

10. 文公十六年 The Sixteen Year Under Lord Civil

宋公子鲍礼于国人，宋饥，竭其粟而贷之。年自七十以上，无不馈诒也，时加羞珍异。

Prince Abalone of Sung was kind to his people. When a famine broke out, he gave out all his grains for charity. All those over 70 years of age had a share besides seasonal delicacies.

11. 宣公二年 The Second Year of Lord Clare

人谁无过？过而能改，善莫大焉。

To err is human, and to reform divine.

12. 宣公十二年 The Twelfth Year of Lord Clare

民生在勤，勤则不匮。

People's livelihood counts on diligence; diligence rears affluence.

13. 宣公十五年 The Fifteenth Year of Lord Clare

谚曰："高下在心。"川泽纳污，山薮藏疾，瑾瑜匿瑕，国君含垢，天之道也。

As a proverb says, "What is high or low is in your heart. Rivers and marshes harbor mud; mountains and bushes harbor disasters; jewels harbor flaws. Therefore, a ruler stands disgrace, as is the Word of Heaven.

14. 成公二年 The Second Year Under Lord Ch'eng

礼以行义，义以生利，利以平民，政之大节也。

Propriety embodies righteousness, righteousness results in profit, and profit settles people, which is the principle of administration.

15. 成公十二年 The Twelve Year Under Lord Ch'eng

同恤灾危，备救凶患……有渝此盟，明神殛之，俾队其师，无克胙国。

They survived the same famine scourge, rescuing each other…If a state violates the covenant, God will condemn it, subverting its troops and destroying it.

16. 成公十五年 The Fifteenth Year Under Lord Ch'eng

诸侯将见子臧于王而立之，子臧辞曰："《前志》有之，曰：'圣达节，次守节，下失节。'为君，非吾节也。虽不能圣，敢失守乎？"遂逃，奔宋。

A vassal suggested Sir Tsang present himself before the king to be appointed as Lord of Tsao. Declining, Sir Tsang replied, "As has been said, a saint communes with rituals; a lower man abides by rituals; the lowest ignores rituals. Trying to reign a state is against rituals. Though not a saint, dare I ignore rituals?" So saying, he fled to Sung.

17. 成公十六年 The Sixteenth Year Under Lord Ch'eng

德以施惠，刑以正邪，详以事神，义以建利，礼以顺时，信以守物。

Virtue is for benevolence, penalty for rectification, piety for God-serving, righteousness for profit, ritual for timing, and faith for maintenance.

18. 襄公十年 The Tenth Year of Lord Hsiang

子产曰：众怒难犯，专欲难成，合二难以安国，危之道也。

Tsuchan said: An angry multitude one should not offend; an arbitrary desire leads nowhere. With these two, it is hard to settle the state; it is a peril.

19. 襄公十一年 The Eleventh Year of Lord Hsiang

秋七月，同盟于亳。范宣子曰："不慎，必失诸侯。诸侯道敝而无成，能无贰乎？"乃盟。载书曰："凡我同盟，毋蕴年，毋壅利……救灾患……或间兹命，司慎、司盟，名山、名川，群神、群祀，先王、先公，七姓十二国之祖，明神殛之，俾失其民，队命亡氏，踣其国家。"

In Seventh Moon, Autumn, an alliance was formed in Po. Sir Clare of Fan said: "Carelessness causes the loss of vassals. Can the vassals, tired and failing, have no dissents?" Then came an oath. According to the covenant, "No allies are allowed to stock up when a disaster falls, nor can they monopolize mountains and rivers… Help one another in times of disaster… If someone violates the covenant, inspectors, guardians, all gods, ghosts, spirits and deities of great mountains and rivers, all lords and forefathers, sires of the seven clans, and ancestors of the twelve kingdoms, will curse him, kill him, and expedite the loss of his people and the subjugation of his state."

20. 襄公十三年 The Thirteen Year of Lord Hsiang

让，礼之主也。

Humbleness is the lord of the rite.

21. 襄公二十二年 The Twenty-Second Year of Lord Hsiang

君人执信，臣人执共，忠、信、笃、敬，上下同之。

A lord should trust and officials should show respect. Loyalty, credit, honesty and faith should be kept by both lord and officials.

22. 襄公二十五年 The Twenty-Fifth Year of Lord Hsiang

君民者，岂以陵民？社稷是主。

How can a lord bully his people? Managing the state is his job.

23. 襄公二十九年 The Twenty-Ninth Year of Lord Hsiang

司城氏贷而不书，为大夫之无者贷。宋无饥人。

Sir Rare the Builder lent his grains to others without asking for IOU, and he also lent in name of officials who did not lend. So no Sung people went hungry.

24. 襄公三十年 The Thirtieth Year of Lord Hsiang

晋人、齐人、宋人、卫人、郑人、曹人、莒人、邾人、滕人、薛人、杞人、小邾人会于澶渊，宋灾故。

Chin, Ch'i, Sung, Watch, Cheng, Ts'ao, Chü, Chu, T'eng, Hsüeh, Ch'ee and Lesser Chu, these states met in Calm Pool (Ch'anyüan), discussing how to help Sung to fight the disaster.

25. 昭公四年 The Forth Year Under Lord Glare

苟利社稷，死生以之。

My life may be sacrificed to benefit the state.

26. 昭公五年 The Forth Year Under Lord Glare

为政者不赏私劳，不罚私怨。

A ruler does not reward his favored one nor punish his feud.

27. 昭公十年 The Tenth Year Under Lord Glare

义，利之本也。蕴利生孽。

Righteousness is the base of profit; amassing profits gives rise to evils.

28. 昭公二十年 The Twentieth Year Under Lord Glare

郑子产有疾，谓子大叔曰："我死，子必为政。唯有德者能以宽服民，其次莫如猛。夫火烈，民望而畏之，故鲜死焉；水懦弱，民狎而玩之，则多死焉，故宽难。"……仲尼曰："善哉！政宽则民慢，慢则纠之以猛。猛则民残，残则施之以宽。宽以济猛，猛以济宽，政是以和。"

Tsuchan, who was ill in Cheng, told Sir Tashu, "After my death you will be appointed premier. Only a virtuous person can be so lenient that people will obey. Without virtue, nothing would be more severe than leniency. As fire appears fierce, so people are afraid of it and few die of it; as water is mild, one may play with it and many get drowned. Therefore, it is hard to administer a lenient government."… Confucius exclaimed, "Good! Too lenient a government will result in people's negligence and in turn the negligence will induce the severity of ruling. If a government is too severe, people will be tortured and reversely, if people are tortured, leniency should come. If leniency and severity can complement each other, a government will run smoothly."

29. 昭公二十五年 The Twenty-Fifth Year Under Lord Glare

将求于人，则先下之，礼之善物也。

When asking for a favor, be humble, as is the right way to do things.

众怒不可蓄也，蓄而弗治，将蕴。蕴蓄，民将生心；生心，同求将合。

The multitude's anger shall not accrue; if accruing without being handled properly, anger will rise. As anger accrues, people will revolt, and those with the same mind will unite.

30. 哀公元年 The First Year of Lord Sad

在国，天有灾疠，亲巡其孤寡而共其乏困。

During his reign, once disasters or plagues fell, he would tour to comfort orphans and widows and help them out of pains and poverty.

31. 哀公七年 The Seventh Year of Lord Sad

小所以事大，信也。大所以保小，仁也。背大国，不信；伐小国，不仁。民保于城，城保于德，失二德者，危，将焉保?

A small state serves a large one with credit. A large state protects a small one with benevolence. Betraying a large state is discredited; invading a small state is malevolent. People are protected by cities; cities are protected by virtues. losing the two virtues, how can a state keep safe in danger?

32. 春秋左传正义 · 昭公六年 Commentary on *Tso's Annals*: The Sixth Year Under Lord Glare

《周礼》："司刑掌五刑之法，以丽万民之罪，墨罪五百，劓罪五百，宫罪五百，刖罪五百，杀罪五百。"据此二文，虽王者相变，条数不同，皆是豫制刑矣。而云"临事制刑，不豫设法"者，圣王虽制刑法，举其大纲，但共犯一法，情有浅深，或轻而难原，或重而可恕，临其时事，议其重轻，虽依准旧条，而断有出入，不豫设定法，告示下民，令不测其浅深，常畏威而惧罪也。

The Rites of Chough says, "The Department of Justice has five types of punishments for all. Each of the five types includes tattoinfront for five hundred crimes, cutoff of nose for five hundred crimes, castration for five hundred crimes, cutoff of feet for five hundred crimes and decapitation for five hundred crimes." According to the set crimes, although a sovereign may have some specific amendments, the articles have been drafted in advance. The usual saying "we can temporarily make a penal law without preset ones" actually expresses a legal viewpoint that although a sage sovereign makes criminal law, he can only give some principles. A similar case of law offence may be different in their respective degree of stringency. Some light crimes may not be pardoned but some heavy crimes can. Occasionally, there are some legal cases which may cause an argument about whether heavy punishment should be imposed or not. Though all legal cases may be judged according to set penal rules, a judge's adjudication may sometimes be different from the previously set ones. Tell the people what has been done instead of letting them know the real depth of the penal punishment and they will be afraid to commit crimes.

33. 春秋左传正义·昭公二十九年 Commentary on *Tso's Annals*: The Twenty-Ninth Year Under Lord Glare

贵者执其权柄，贱者畏其威严，贵贱尊卑不愆，此乃所谓度也。

The noble hold the power and the low are awed by the power. If neither of them deviates from their respective role, it is called proper devoir.

第二节 《史记》
Section 2 *Records of the Grand Historian*

1. 五帝本纪 Records of the Five Lords

黄帝者，少典之子，姓公孙，名曰轩辕。生而神灵，弱而能言，幼而徇齐，长而敦敏，成而聪明。轩辕之时，神农氏世衰。诸侯相侵伐，暴虐百姓，而神农氏弗能征。于是轩辕乃习用干戈，以征不享，诸侯咸来宾从。而蚩尤最为暴，莫能伐。炎帝欲侵陵诸侯，诸侯咸归轩辕。轩辕乃修德振兵，治五气，艺五种，抚万民，度四方，教熊罴貔貅貙虎，以与炎帝战于阪泉之野。三战，然后得其志。蚩尤作乱，不用帝命。于是黄帝乃征师诸侯，与蚩尤战于涿鹿之野，遂禽杀蚩尤。而诸侯咸尊轩辕为天子，代神农氏，是为黄帝。天下有不顺者，黄帝从而征之，平者去之，披山通道，未尝宁居。

Lord Yellow, son of Small Land (Shaodian), named Cartshaft (Hsüanyüan), surnamed Lordson (Kongsun), born divine, could talk while an infant, grew from a smart baby into an honest and quick-witted teenager, and then into an intelligent man. At the time of Cartshaft, Farmer God's Tribe began to decline and he could not stop his vassals from fighting each other and harming the folk, therefore Cartshaft rose to train troops and subdue vassals who refused to pay tributes. All surrendered except Bug Wart (Ch'iyou), who was the most brutal. When Lord Fire (Yanti) bullied his vassals, they came to Cartshaft. Cartshaft promoted virtues and drilled troops, studied weather, grew crops, measured land, appeased the folk, and trained bears, pinchoofs, leopards and tigers for a fight. Cartshaft fought with Lord Fire at Slopespring (Banch'uan), and fulfilled his will after a few battles. Then Bug Wart rose in revolt, disobeying the lord. So Cartshaft led his vassals to fight with Bug Wart at Flowdeer (Chuolu), captured and killed him there. So all the vassals came to Cartshaft and esteemed him as king to replace God Farmer, hence Lord Yellow. Lord Yellow went on to subjugate every unyielding tribe and conquered one after another while cutting through mountains and blazing trails wherever he went, without being settled.

仁而威，惠而信，修身而天下服。

Benevolence and dignity, favor and faith are what subjugates the world.

于是舜乃至于文祖，谋于四岳，辟四门，明通四方耳目。命十二牧论帝德，行厚德，远佞人，则蛮夷率服。

Then Hibiscus reached Ancestral Temple, consulted with the four mountains, opened the four gates, and smoothed links with four directions. He ordered the 12 governors to discuss the virtues of kingship: conduct deeds of great virtues, stay away from ill-meant flatterers, and the remote peoples will come over.

2. 殷本纪 Records of Yin

人视水见形，视民知治不。

Looking into water, you see how you look; looking into people, you know how they're ruled.

3. 秦始皇本纪 Records of Emperor First of Ch'in

牧民之道，务在安之而已。天下虽有逆行之臣，必无响应之助矣。

To shepherd people is to settle them. Once settled, none of them will support rebels if any.

4. 高祖本纪 Records of Pang Liu, Highroot of Han

（刘邦）召诸县父老豪桀曰："父老苦秦苛法久矣，诽谤者族，偶语者弃市。吾与诸侯约，先入关者王之，吾当王关中。与父老约，法三章耳：杀人者死，伤人及盗抵罪。馀悉除去秦法。诸吏人皆案堵如故。凡吾所以来，为父老除害，非有所侵暴，无恐！且吾所以还军霸上，待诸侯至而定约束耳。"乃使人与秦吏行县乡邑，告谕之。秦人大喜，争持牛羊酒食献飨军士。沛公又让不受，曰："仓粟多，非乏，不欲费人。"人又益喜，唯恐沛公不为秦王。

Pang Liu summoned the folks and heroes from various counties, saying: "The folks have suffered from the harsh laws of Ch'in for so long. Those who slander the emperor will have his clan destroyed; those who meet to discuss the court will have their heads cut off in the market." The lords and I agreed that he who first came through the pass would be king, so I should now be king. As has been agreed with the elders that there are only three articles of law: a murderer shall die, and he who hurts and robs shall be punished, commensurate with the crime. The rest of the Ch'in laws are abolished. Officials and folks must live in peace. This is why I am here to expel harms for my folks and elders, no bullying, don't be afraid. As now I've returned to Pashang, I'm waiting for the princes to come and work out a common discipline." Pang Liu sent his people and officials to patrol the counties and towns to spread his announcement. The people of Ch'in were very happy and rushed to offer their cattle and sheep, wine and food to his soldiers. And Pang Liu humbled himself and declined the offer, saying: "I have a lot of millet in barns, a large supply, so you keep all that for yourselves." The people were very happy, afraid Pang Liu would not be their king.

高祖置酒洛阳南宫。高祖曰："列侯诸将无敢隐朕，皆言其情。吾所以有天下者何？项氏之所以失天下者何？"高起、王陵对曰："陛下慢而侮人，项羽仁而爱人。然陛下使人攻城略地，所降下者因以予之，与天下同利也。项羽妒贤嫉能，有功者害之，贤者疑之，战胜而不予人功，得地而不予人利，此所以失天下也。"

Pang Liu set up a banquet at South Palace in Loshine, saying: "You lords and generals do not hide from me, please tell me the truth. Why did I win the world and Why did Yu Hsiang lose the world?" Ch'i Kao and Ling Wang replied, "Your Majesty was arrogant and insulting while Yu Hsiang was kind and loving. However, when Your Majesty sent troops to capture a city, the place he had taken he distributed to the soldiers and shared the benefits with the rest of the world. Yu Hsiang envied and framed up against the meritorious, and suspected the virtuous. When he won a battle, he did not give reward, and when he obtained a land, he did not share it. That was why he lost the world."

太史公曰：夏之政忠，忠之敝，小人以野，故殷人承之以敬。敬之敝，小人以鬼，故周人承之以文。文之敝，小人以僿，故救僿莫若以忠。三王之道若循环，终而复始。周、秦之间，可谓文敝矣。秦政不改，反酷刑法，岂不缪乎？故汉兴，承敝易变，使人不倦，得天统矣。

Grand Historiographer said: It was Hsia's politics to value loyalty. The malpractice in loyalty was the rudeness of the common, so Yin's people turned respectful. The shortcoming of respect is that people believe in ghosts and gods, so Chough's people replaced it with etiquette. And the shortcoming of etiquette is that the people are insincere. So there is nothing better to correct insincerity than loyalty. Hsia, Shang, and Chough, these three ages of kings made a cycle in governance, ending only to begin. Between Chough and Ch'in, the drawback was the excessive attention to etiquette. Ch'in's politics did not change this kind of malpractice, on the contrary, it did make the criminal law more severe, isn't this a mistake? So the rise of Han, although having inherited the drawbacks of the previous period, did not make people tired, and Han must have got the Word of Heaven.

5. 货殖列传 Biography of Merchants

故曰："仓廪实而知礼节，衣食足而知荣辱。"礼生于有而废于无。故君子富，好行其德；小人富，以适其力。渊深而鱼生之，山深而兽往之，人富而仁义附焉。富者得执益彰，失执则客无所之，以而不乐，夷狄益甚。谚曰："千金之子，不死于市。"此非空言也。故曰："天下熙熙，皆为利来；天下攘攘，皆为利往。"夫千乘之王，万家之侯，百室之君，尚犹患贫，而况匹夫编户之民乎！

As is said: "Barns and granaries full, people become polite; food and clothing enough, known is honor or shame." Rites come out of wealth and vanish in poverty. Therefore, a gentleman, if rich, does what is good; a villain, if rich, does what he would. Fish teem where rivers are deep; beasts lurk where mountains are high; rich men go with benevolence and righteousness. Power gained, a rich man is prominent; power lost, he has no guests coming, so he will be unhappy, as is more obvious with barbarians. As a saying goes, “A bounteous millionaire will not die in the fair.” This is no empty talk. Therefore it is said, “All in the world hustle for profits; all in the world bustle for interests.” Even a king with thousands of chariots, vassals with myriads of houses, and archons with hundreds of chambers are worried about poverty, let alone the households of the common registered!

《周书》曰：“农不出则乏其食，工不出则乏其事，商不出则三宝绝，虞不出则财匮少。”财匮少而山泽不辟矣。此四者，民所衣食之原也。原大则饶，原小则鲜。上则富国，下则富家。贫富之道，莫之夺予，而巧者有馀，拙者不足。故太公望封于营丘，地潟卤，人民寡，于是太公劝其女功，极技巧，通鱼盐，则人物归之，繦至而辐凑。故齐冠带衣履天下，海岱之间敛袂而往朝焉。

The Book of Chough said: “If farmers have no yield, there will be a shortage of food; if craftsmen don’t manufacture, there will be no storage of implements; if merchants don’t exchange, there will be no trading of treasures; if conservators don’t exploit, there will be no supply of resources.” Resources being rare, forests and moors remain intact. These are the four sources of people’s food and clothing. Rich with them, a state becomes rich; short of them, it becomes poor. They can enrich a state as well as a family. The way to poverty or wealth does not lie in taking or giving, simply the wise have more and the foolish have less. Thus, Great Grand, faced with the saline fields and a small population in Camp Hillock, his fief, encouraged women to weave, promoted craftsmanship, and boosted trades of fish and salt, so people and commodities gathered around him, like strings of coins or aggregating spokes. Thus, Ch’i’s hats, laces, clothes and shoes gained worldwide fame, and all between the sea and Mt. Arch came to worship him.

6. 商君列传 Biography of Yang Shang

民不可与虑始而可与乐成。论至德者不和于俗，成大功者不谋于众。是以圣人苟可以强国，不法其故；苟可以利民，不循其礼。

You should not plan with the folks beforehand though you can share with them your success. He who talks about the highest virtue does not go with the worldly, and those who do greatest things do not discuss with others. Therefore, so long as a sage can strengthen the state, he does not have to follow old ways; so long as he can benefit the people, he does not have to follow etiquette.

非其位而居之曰贪位，非莫名而有之曰贪名。

Taking a position one should not take is called hankering after power; enjoying a reputation one does not deserve is called hankering after fame.

7. 循吏列传 Biography of Good Officials

李离者，晋文公之理也。过听杀人，自拘当死。文公曰："官有贵贱，罚有轻重。下吏有过，非子之罪也。"李离曰："臣居官为长，不与吏让位；受禄为多，不与下分利。今过听杀人，傅其罪下吏，非所闻也。"辞不受令。文公曰："子则自以为有罪，寡人亦有罪邪？"李离曰："理有法，失刑则刑，失死则死。公以臣能听微决疑，故使为理。今过听杀人，罪当死。"遂不受令，伏剑而死。

Li Li, a judge appointed by Lord Civil of Chin, made an error in interrogation, which cost a life. He arrested himself for death penalty. Lord Civil said: "Punishment varies according to positions and ranks. It was your subordinates' fault, not yours." Li Li declined it, saying: "I, a high court judge, never give my position to my subordinates; I earn a great deal, but never give them a bit. Now someone died due to my fault, but I should shuffle blame onto my subordinates—such a case I have never heard of." Lord Civil reiterated: "You claim your guilt, then should I take the blame as well?" Li Li replied: "A judge gives his verdict based on laws. If he gives a wrong sentence, he should accept the penalty, and if he causes an innocent man to die, he should pay with his life. Your Lordship appointed me judge because of my good observation in interrogation and capability for tough cases. Now an innocent man died due to my fault, so I should die." Without accepting the lord's pardon, he cut his own throat with his sword.

8. 酷吏列传 Biography of Cruel Officials

老氏称："上德不德，是以有德；下德不失德，是以无德。法令滋章，盗贼多有。"太史公曰：信哉是言也！法令者治之具，而非制治清浊之源也。昔天下之网尝密矣，然奸伪萌起，其极也，上下相遁，至于不振。当是之时，吏治若救火扬沸，非武健严酷，恶能胜其任而愉快乎？言道德者，溺其职矣。故曰："听讼，吾犹人也，必也使无讼乎！""下士闻道大笑之。"非虚言也。汉兴，破觚而为圆，斫雕而为朴，网漏于吞舟之鱼，而吏治蒸蒸，不至于奸，黎民艾安。由是观之，在彼不在此。

Laocius said: "The top virtue shows no virtue, hence virtue; the low virtue keeps its virtue, hence no virtue. The top virtue does nothing and keeps nothing. The more severe the law is, the more thieves there sway. Grand Historiographer said that these are correct. Laws are tools to administrate a state, not those to administrate well or not. Once, the laws were detailed, but fraudulence frequently occurred, during the depths of which, the officials passed the buck to each other, as a result the empire declined. At that time, officials used laws just like adding fuel to fire. If tough measures couldn't be taken, how could one be competent and content? In such a case, those who prattle about ethics lose their duty. Therefore, Confucius said: "In oyer and terminer, I am just like others. We must do everything to have no lawsuit." Laocius said: "A lower man, hearing the Word, laughs at it." It is no empty talk. When Han rose, squares were chopped into circles and ornateness made into simplicity, and the net of laws was made sparse as if it could drop boat-swallowing fish, and the governance was so effective that fraudulence was reduced and stability assured. From such a perspective, the key to administrating a state is ethics instead of harsh laws.

9. 屈原贾生列传 Biography of Yüan Ch'ü and E Chia

人君无愚智贤不肖，莫不欲求忠以自为，举贤以自佐，然亡国破家相随属，而圣君治国累世不见者，其所谓忠者不忠，而所谓贤者不贤也。

No lord, be he stupid, wise, noble or despicable, does not want to have loyal officials work for him or find noble men to assist him. However, states perish one by one while a state well governed by a wise lord is rarely seen for generations. The reason is that those thought to be loyal are not loyal, and those believed to be noble are not noble.

10. 日者列传 Biography of Augurs

官非其任不处也，禄非其功不受也。

Not competent, do not take the position; not worthy, do not accept the salary.

才不贤而托官位，利上奉，妨贤者处，是窃位也。

Having no talent but muddling on, hankering after salaries and hindering talents in their appointments, this is called stealing official power.

11. 淮阴侯列传 Marquess of Huaishade

故知者决之断也，疑者事之害也，审豪厘之小计，遗天下之大数，智诚知之，决弗敢行者，百事之祸也。

Wise men make decisions, and hesitation is the scourge in doing things. It is a root of troubles if one is bound to trivialities while neglecting the big plan, knowing something should be done but daring not get down to it.

12. 齐悼惠王世家 Aristocratic Family of Prince Mournboon of Ch'i

当断不断，反受其乱。

Crush the trouble, or be crushed by it.

13. 赵世家 Aristocratic Family of Chao

仁者爱万物。

The benevolent love all.

14. 楚世家 Aristocratic Family of Ch'u

君蚤自图，无取辱焉。众怒如水火，不可救也。

Be prepared early in case you bring shame to yourself. A crowd may burst with anger like water and fire, and once it bursts, it is out of control.

15. 楚元王世家 Aristocratic Family of King One of Ch'u

国之将兴，必有祯祥，君子用而小人退；国之将亡，贤人隐，乱臣贵。

There must be some auspices when a country is going to prosper. Meantime, when gentlemen are promoted, snobs will go off; when a country is going to perish, gentlemen will retreat and traitors swagger.

安危在出令，存亡在所任。

A country's peril or safety depends on the sovereign's decrees and a country's subjugation or existence hinges on the policies he adopts.

16. 曹相国世家 Aristocratic Family of Premier Ts'ao

治道贵清静而民自定。

A stable state, a stable people.

且高帝与萧何定天下，法令既明，今陛下垂拱，参等守职，遵而勿失，不亦可乎？

Highroot, aided by Ho Hsiao, settled the land and the laws and decrees were clearly promulgated to the public. Now Your Majesty can govern the country with inaction and we subjects try to do our duty without negligence. It is a good thing to do, isn't it?

17. 礼书 Rites

明道而均分之，时使而诚爱之，则下应之如景响。有不由命者，然后俟之以刑，则民知罪矣。

Teach the people, regarding them equally and caring them sincerely, and then the people will follow like a shadow or an echo. Should someone disobey, punish them properly, and then the people will know they are wrong.

18. 太史公自序 Grand Historiographer's Preface

法家不别亲疏，不殊贵贱，一断于法。

All legal cases shall be decided by law irrespective of kindred or ranks.

第三节 《汉书》
Section 3 *The History of Han*

1. 景帝纪 Record of Emperor Scene

人不患其不知，患其为诈也；不患其不勇，患其为暴也；不患其不富，患其亡厌也。其唯廉士，寡欲易足。今訾算十以上乃得宦，廉士算不必众。有市籍不得宦，无訾又不得宦，朕甚愍之。訾算四得宦，亡令廉士久失职，贪夫长利。

Do not worry someone's not wise, but his fraudulence you should worry about; do not worry someone's not brave, but his brutality you should worry about; do not worry someone's not rich, but venality you should worry about. Only a clean man's desire is easy to be satisfied. The stipulation requires that one should possess a hundred thousand to become an official, but this does not apply to those who are clean. Those who have their own businesses should not be officials and those who have no money should not be officials. I feel so sorry about that, so now I give the order: men who have but forty thousand can become officials, lest clean men get no position while greedy ones graft there for long.

2. 食货志 Foods and Goods

种谷必杂五种，以备灾害。田中不得有树，用妨五谷。力耕数耘，收获如寇盗之至。

Diversification of crops is advocated against possible disasters; trees must not be planted in the field in case crops are harmed. Tilling hard raking well, and harvesting as fast as if robbers were coming.

又曰籴甚贵伤民，甚贱伤农；民伤则离散，农伤则国贫。

A high price of grain will harm residents; a low price of grain will adversely affect peasants. If badly affected, residents will go away; if badly influenced, peasants will make the state poor.

3. 陈胜项籍传 Biography of Sheng Ch'en and Chi Hsiang

先发制人，后发制于人。

Attack preemptively, and you win; respond passively, and you lose.

4. 楚元王传 Biography of Chiao Liu, First Prince of Ch'u

谗邪之所以并进者，由上多疑心，既已用贤人行善政，如或谮之，则贤人退而善政还。

The reason why the slanderous and wicked can step into the court is largely due to an emperor's suspicion. If talents who have been appointed to carry out good policies are framed, they will quit. Consequently, good governance will be suspended.

治乱荣辱之端，在所信任；信任既贤，在于坚固而不移。

Prosperity or disturbance, glory or shame lies in trust. If talents are to be trusted, an emperor should trust them without hesitation.

5. 张释之传 Biography of Shihchih Chang

廷尉，天下之平也，壹倾，天下用法皆为之轻重，民安所措其手足？

The Minister of Justice is a balance for the whole country. Once tilting, he won't enforce law improperly. In that case, how can people be settled and reassured?

6. 董仲舒传 Biography of Chungshu Tung

天道之大者在阴阳。阳为德，阴为刑；刑主杀而德主生。

The greatness of the Word lies in Shade (negative) and Shine (positive), with Shine as virtue constituting life, and Shade as penalty constituting death.

毋以日月为功，实试贤能为上，量材而授官，录德而定位，则廉耻殊路，贤不肖异处矣。

One's merit shall not depend on the period of his service. He should be judged by his capabilities; his status and ranks should be determined by his virtue and performance. Thus, a clear distinction shall be made between honesty and impudicity. So the virtuous shall not be mixed with those shameless ones.

法天而立道。

Modeled on Heaven, show the Word to the world.

7. 王褒传 Biography of Pao Wang

圣主必待贤臣而弘功业，俊士亦俟明主以显其德。

A lord relies on his sage officials for great exploits; a talent needs a wise lord to reveal his virtues.

8. 杨胡朱梅云传 Biography of Wangsun Yang, Chien Hu, Yün Chu, Fu Mei, and Ch'ang Yün

上不能匡主，下亡以益民，皆尸位素餐。

He who who cannot uphold his lord or serve the people is called a fathead doing nothing.

9. 陈汤传 Biography of T'ang Ch'en

记人之功，忘人之过。

Give him credit for the good he's done and forgive him if he is wrong.

10. 王贡两龚鲍传 Biography of Chi Wang, Yü Kung, Sheng Kung, She Kung and Hsuan Pao

又有七死：酷吏殴杀，一死也；治狱深刻，二死也；冤陷亡辜，三死也；盗贼横发，四死也；怨仇相残，五死也；岁恶饥饿，六死也；时气疾疫，七死也。民有七亡而无一得，欲望国安，诚难；民有七死而无一生，欲望刑措，诚难。

And there are seven kinds of death: cruel officials' beating and killing, this the first; trying cases harshly, this the second; wronging the innocent, this the third; robberies everywhere, this the fourth; enemies killing each other, this the fifth; a famine and starvation, this the sixth; a rampant plague, this the seventh. There are seven kinds of death but not any gains, so it is really difficult to have a peaceful state. There are seven kinds of loss of lives without hope of survival, so it is really difficult to enforce law.

治天下者当用天下之心为心，不得自专快意而已也。上之皇天见谴，下之黎庶怨恨，次之谏诤之臣，陛下苟欲自薄而厚恶臣，天下犹不听也。

To manage a state, a king must care what people care. He should not go ahead with his own fancies. With God's curse, people's resentment and ministers' admonitions, even if a king wants to reduce his own influence and increase evil ministers' power, nobody will listen to him.

11. 宣元六王传 Biography of Six Kings under the Reigns of Emperor Piousbroad and Emperor Piousfirst of Han

夫福善之门莫美于和睦，患咎之首莫大于内离。

In terms of goodness, nothing is better than harmony; in terms of harmfulness, nothing is worse than internal conflicts.

12. 傅喜传 Biography of Hsi Fu

百万之众，不如一贤，故秦行千金以间廉颇，汉散万金以疏亚父。

A talent is better than a million troops. Therefore, the State of Ch'in spent thousands of gold trying to cause discord between Lianpo and the State of Chao, Highroot of Han alienated Tseng Fan at the cost of tens of thousands of gold.

第四节　《贞观政要》
Section 4　*Governance of Right Done*

1. 君道 Sovereignty

贞观初，太宗谓侍臣曰："为君之道，必须先存百姓。若损百姓以奉其身，犹割股以啖腹，腹饱而身毙。若安天下，必须先正其身，未有身正而影曲，上治而下乱者。朕每思伤其身者不在外物，皆由嗜欲以成其祸。若耽嗜滋味，玩悦声色，所欲既多，所损亦大，既妨政事，又扰生人。且复出一非理之言，万姓为之解体，怨讟既作，离叛亦兴。朕每思此，不敢纵逸。”谏议大夫魏徵对曰：“古者圣哲之主，皆亦近取诸身，故能远体诸物。昔楚聘詹何，问其治国之要，詹何对以修身之术。楚王又问治国何如？詹何曰：‘未闻身治而国乱者。’陛下所明，实同古义。”

In the first year of Right Done, Grandsire of T'ang said to his officials: "The first and foremost of a sovereign is to sustain people. If he sacrifices his people for his own interest, it is very much like cutting his thigh to feed his stomach. When his stomach is fed, he is dying. To settle the world, a sovereign must first straighten himself. There has never been a distorted shadow from a straight figure or upheavals down from peace above. I often think what ruins the body is excessive desires, not external things. Too much indulgence in gourmet, music and beauties can cause too many desires and ruins, harmful to both political affairs and people. With improper words from the lord, people would go asunder, and there would arise dissents and groans, and rebellions. Whenever I think of this, I dared not be given to comforts and luxuries." Remonstrant Cheng Wei replied: "All wise ancient kings would first introspect the conduct of themselves, so they could understand things afar. King Lush of Ch'u employed Ho Chan to ask him about the essence of governance." Chan replied with a matter of self-cultivation. King Lush asked about governance again. Chan answered: "I have never heard that a king is well cultivated but his state is riotous. Your Majesty's idea is in accordance with that of the ancient times."

生骄逸之端，必践危亡之地。

With a symptom of arrogance and extravagance, a state will be surely dragged into danger.

2. 政体 Governance

贞观初，太宗谓萧瑀曰："朕少好弓矢，自谓能尽其妙。近得良弓十数，以示弓工。乃曰：'皆非良材也。'朕问其故。工曰：'木心不正，则脉理皆邪，弓虽刚劲而遣箭不直，非良弓也。'朕始悟焉。朕以弧矢定四方，用弓多矣，而犹不得其理。况朕有天下之日浅，得为理之意，固未及于弓，弓犹失之，而况于理乎？"自是诏京官五品以上，更宿中书内省。每召见，皆赐坐与语，询访外事，务知百姓利害、政教得失焉。

In the first year of Right Done, Grandsire of T'ang said to Yü Hsiao: "When I was young, I was fond of archery and I thought I knew a lot about bows and arrows. Recently I have got several great ones, and I showed them to a master. I was told that they were not made of top wood. I asked why. He replied: 'The duramen is not well-positioned, so its veins are not straight. Bows made of it can be powerful, but they cannot shoot straight, so they are not good bows." I realized that. I won the world with bows and arrows and have used many. However, I have not got the knack of knowing them, let alone my reign that is quite short up to now. My knowledge for governance cannot be more than that about bows and arrows. My knowledge of bows and arrows is not totally correct, let alone that of governance." From then on, the emperor met fifth rank officials in the capital regularly and moved to stay for the night in the Secretariat. For every gathering, he offered them seats and talked with them, asking about the situation outside the palace. In this way, he could well know how the people's situation and the gains and losses of management.

凡大事皆起于小事，小事不论，大事又将不可救。社稷倾危，莫不由此。

All big events are caused by small ones. If small events are neglected, it will be hard to amend when they develop into big ones. There is no other way for a state to perish.

贞观七年，太宗与秘书监魏徵从容论自古理政得失，因曰："当今大乱之后，造次不可致理。"徵曰："不然。凡人在危困则忧死亡，忧死亡则思理，思理则易教。然则乱后易教，犹饥人易食也。"太宗曰："善人为邦百年，然后胜残去杀。大乱之后，将求致理，宁可造次而望乎？"徵曰："此据常人，不在圣哲。若圣哲施化，上下同心，人应如响，不疾而速，期月而可，信不为难，三年成功，犹谓其晚。"太宗以为然。封德彝等对曰："三代以后，人渐浇讹，故秦任法律，汉杂霸道，皆欲理而不能，岂能理而不欲？若信魏徵所说，恐败乱国家。"徵曰："五帝、三王，不易人而理。行帝道则帝，行王道则王，在于当时所理，化之而已。考之载籍，可得而知。昔黄帝与蚩尤七十馀战，其乱甚矣，既胜之后，便致太平。九黎乱德，颛顼征之，既克之后，不失其理。桀为乱虐，而汤放之，在汤之代，既致太平。纣为无道，武王伐之，成王之代，亦致太平。若言人渐浇讹，不及纯朴，至今应悉为鬼魅，宁可复得而教化耶？"德彝等无以难之，然咸以为不可。太宗每力行不倦，数年间，海内康宁，突厥破灭，因谓群臣曰："贞观初，人皆异论，云当今必不可行帝道、王道，惟魏徵劝我。既从其言，不过数载，遂得华夏安宁，远戎宾服。突厥自古以来，常为中国勍敌，今酋长并带刀宿卫，部落皆袭衣冠。使我遂至于此，皆魏徵之力也。"顾谓徵曰："玉虽有美质，在于石间，不值良工琢磨，与瓦砾不别。若遇良工，即为万代之宝。朕虽无美质，为公所切磋，劳公约朕以仁义，弘朕以道德，使朕功业至此，公亦足为良工尔。"

In the 7th year of Right Done, Grandsire of T'ang talked to Imperial Inspector Cheng Wei about gains and losses of governance from ancient times. The emperor said: "Now, we cannot long for great peace after a great turbulence." Wei relied: "No. When people are in danger, they fear death, which means they long for peace. Their longing for peace makes it easy to enlighten them by education. It is the same as hunger makes people easy to be fed." Grandsire said: "It takes 100 years for the wise to realize good governance. How can great peace be made quickly after a great disorder?" Wei relied: "What Your Majesty mentioned only applies to the ordinary, not saints. If enlightenment is done by the wise with efforts from all, people can respond as fast as an echo does.

It can be achieved in a month, not so hard; it can be called late if achieved in three years." Grandsire agreed. Te-e Feng and other officials held quite different ideas, and he said to the emperor: "After Hsia, Shang and Chough, people became wicked and crafty. So Ch'in adopted the method of governance by law and Han adopted the method of governance by combining law and benevolence. Both intended to enlighten all, but they failed. If Your Majesty believes in Wei's words, our country will be thrown into chaos." Wei answered: "We can know from history that a reason for great governance by kings and emperors is the implementation of enlightenment by education. Do what a great emperor does, and you can be that emperor; do what a great king does, and you can be that king. Lord Yellow and Wart Bug fought over seventy times. However, order was soon restored after the victory. When Manifold staged an armed rebellion, Plump Head sent out troops to attack the rebel forces. After the suppression, a period of peace and prosperity regained. Stump was cruel and furious. When Hotspring of Shang expelled him, order was soon achieved at the beginning of Hotspring's governance. Chow was tyrannic, and King Martial fought him and King Complete finished him, then the country was in order. If we believe that people are inclined to be evil, they should be wicked ghosts now. How can enlightenment be done?" Though words failed Feng and others, Feng still viewed Wei's idea as unfeasible. Whereas, Grandsire insisted on carrying out Wei's thought. Several years later, the country became peaceful and the once rival Turks came over and pledged allegiance. The emperor said to his officials: "At first, ideas varied for governance. Some thought that it was hard to implement the doings of previous emperors or kings. Only Cheng Wei persuaded me into doing so. Now, our country is peaceful and nations far away submitted themselves to our rule. Turks used to be a very powerful rival. Now, their leader, armed with knives, is my guard. His people wear our clothes. I attribute my achievements to Wei." Turning his head toward Wei, Grandsire said to him: "Nice as it is, jade is mixed with stone. Without an excellent craftsman, there is no difference between stone and jade. With an excellent craftsman, jade can be carved into a priceless jewel. Thanks to your crafting with benevolence and virtue, I can have what I have now. You are a genuine craftsman."

3. 附：直谏 Admonishment

（魏徵言）自古有道之主，以百姓之心为心，故君处台榭，则欲民有栋宇之安；食膏粱，则欲民无饥寒之患；顾嫔御，则欲民有室家之欢。此人主之常道也。

Since ancient times, a good lord has had his people's heart as his own, so when he sits in a pavilion, he wants his people to have a house; when he eats delicious food, he wants to keep his people from hunger; and when he sees concubines, he wants his people have a happy family. This is what a sovereign should do.

4. 君臣鉴戒 Commandments for the Emperor and Officials

任之虽重，信之未笃，则人或自疑。人或自疑，则心怀苟且。心怀苟且，则节义不立。节义不立，则名教不兴。名教不兴而可与固太平之基、保七百之祚，未之有也。

If a talent is appointed to an important position but is not trusted fully, then his or others' suspicion will be aroused. In this case, he may be perfunctory; perfunctory, he will not have good morality; without good morality, he will not set a good example; without a good example, there will not be a good base for good governance, let alone the governance that can consolidate long-term harmony and prosperity.

5. 择官 Appointment

贞观二年，太宗谓侍臣曰："朕每夜恒思百姓间事，或至夜半不寐，惟恐都督、刺史堪养百姓以否。故于屏风上录其姓名，坐卧恒看。在官如有善事，亦具列于名下。朕居深宫之中，视听不能及远，所委者惟都督、刺史。此辈实治乱所系，尤须得人。”

贞观二年，太宗谓右仆射封德彝曰：“致安之本，惟在得人。比来命卿举贤，未尝有所推荐。天下事重，卿宜分朕忧劳，卿既不言，朕将安寄？”

对曰：“臣愚岂敢不尽情？但今所见，未有奇才异能。”

太宗曰：“前代明王使人如器，皆取士于当时，不借才于异代。岂得待梦傅说、逢吕尚然后为政乎？且何代无贤，但患遗而不知耳！”德彝惭赧而退。

In the 2nd year of Right Done, Grandsire said to his officials: “Every night, I think about what happens among people. In sleepless nights, I am worried whether governors can love and protect them. I carve their names on the folding screen and watch them incessantly, sitting or lying. When they do something good, I list it under their name. As I am in the palace, far away from the people, I have to resort to governors and inspectors for people’s welfare. I do need competent officials who determine the country’s security and well-being.”

In the 2nd year of Right Done, Grandsire said to Vice-premier Te-e Feng: “Peace lies in talents. I have asked you to recommend talents, why don’t you recommend someone? I am heavily burdened, and you should share some of my troubles. If you don’t, who should?” Te-e Feng replied: “Dull as I am, how dare I not do my best? The problem is that I have not discovered any.” Grandsire replied:“Ancient kings, like using utensils, employed talents from the present dynasty, not borrowing from other ones. How can I find talents like Yüeh Fu found in a dream or Great Grand bumped into? There are talents in all dynasties, only that we haven’t found them.” Hearing it, Te-e was ashamed and withdrew.

设令此人不能济事，只是才力不及，不为大害。误用恶人，假令强干，为患极多。但乱世惟求其才，不顾其行。太平之时，必须才行俱兼，始可任用。

Suppose a man cannot fulfill his task just because he is not so capable, there will be no great harm. If a wicked man is appointed, even though competent, there will be great harm. But in times of turmoil, talent is first sought and morality is disregarded. In a time of peace, only a man of both talent and morality can be appointed.

贞观十三年，太宗谓侍臣曰："朕闻太平后必有大乱，大乱后必有太平。大乱之后，即是太平之运也。能安天下者，惟在用得贤才。公等既不能知贤，朕又不可遍识，日复一日，无得人之理。今欲令人自举，于事何如？"

魏徵对曰："知人者智，自知者明。知人既以为难，自知诚亦不易。且愚暗之人，皆矜能伐善，恐长浇竞之风，不可令其自举。"

In the 13th year of Right Done, Grandsire said to his ministers: "It is said that there must be upheavals after peace, and peace after upheavals. A peaceful world depends on talents and the use of them. Since you don't know talents and I can't know all, and day after day we see no talents, I would like to release an order of self-recommendation for talents. What do you think of it?" Cheng Wei replied: "He who knows others is smart; he who knows himself is wise. It is no easy job to know others as well as himself. But the foolish and ignorant all praise their own ability and virtue, so self-recommendation, I am afraid, can ignite one's passion to pursue fame and fortune."

因其材以取之，审其能以任之，用其所长，掩其所短。

Select one according to his talent, appoint one based on his competence, make use of what he is good at and avoid what he is short of.

6. 规谏太子 Admonishing a Crown Prince

昔三王之教子，兼四时以齿学；将交发于中外，乃先之以礼乐。乐以移风易俗，礼以安上化人。非有悦于钟鼓，将宣志以和神。宁有怀于玉帛，将克己而庇身。

Of yore, the three kings taught their children with the cycle of four seasons, and thc princes would be led out to be taught rites and music. Music is uscd to improve the society, and rites to stabilize rules and educate the public. Learning music is not out of one's love for music but for one to show his will and calm his mind. Do you want to learn rites to get rich? Just to restrain yourself and assure security.

7. 公平 Fairness

用人但问堪否，岂以新故异情?

The only thing to consider in terms of personnel management is whether talents are qualified or not. How can an appointment have to do with kin or friendship?

惟有才行是任，岂以新旧为差?

Only talent and morality count in personnel management, how can seniority make a difference?

理国要道，在于公平正直。

What is most important of governance is to maintain fairness and integrity.

凡听讼理狱，必原父子之亲，立君臣之义，权轻重之序，测浅深之量。悉其聪明，致其忠爱，然后察之，疑则与众共之。疑则从轻者，所以重之也，故舜命咎繇曰："汝作士，惟刑之恤。"又复加之以三讯，众所善，然后断之。是以为法，参之人情。

Whenever hearing a legal case at court, a judge should consider the kinship between father and son, the hierarchy between lord and subject and then determine the degree of penalty according to the severity of his crime. As a judge, you should make full use of your intelligence, entirely extend your loyalty and love and then have a reflection. If you find something uncertain, discuss it with others. If you find some thing suspicious in a legal case, you should strive to be lenient before making your final decision. Thus Hibiscus said to Moor Potter, "As Minster of Justice, you should be cautious with punishments!" Besides, there is a procedure of "three inquiries" (of ministers, local officials and ordinary people). If everybody thinks it correct, then you can make your final decision, which means that execution of law should take human feelings into consideration.

凡理狱之情，必本所犯之事以为主，不严讯，不旁求，不贵多端，以见聪明，故律正其举劾之法，参伍其辞，所以求实也，非所以饰实也。但当参伍明听之耳，不使狱吏锻炼饰理成辞于手。

When a judge tries a legal case, he should focus on the facts of the crime, not abusing torture or deliberately implicating other crimes or trying to find more implications to show his shrewdness. Thereof, our law specifically stipulates the systems for proof finding, interrogation and cross-examination for legal facts rather than concealing evidences so that more people can be aware to prevent warders from bending the law or forging judicial documents.

8. 慎所好 Caution in Interest

贞观四年，太宗曰："隋炀帝性好猜防，专信邪道，大忌胡人，乃至谓胡床为交床，胡瓜为黄瓜，筑长城以避胡，终被宇文化及使令狐行达杀之。又诛戮李金才，及诸李殆尽，卒何所益？且君天下者，惟须正身修德而已，此外虚事，不足在怀。"

In the fourth year of Right Done, Grandsire of T'ang said: "Emperor Yang of Sui was suspicious by nature and believed in evil ways. He was particularly wary of Huns, calling a Hun stool a stoop and Hun cucumber a cucumber, and building great walls to check them. Emperor Yang was killed by Hsingta Linghu ordered by Huachi Yüwen. He killed General Chintsai Li and people bearing the surname of Li were all but massacred. What's the use of that? What a sovereign needs to do is to cultivate himself, and all others are but nothing.

9. 慎言语 Caution in Speech

贞观八年，太宗谓侍臣曰："言语者君子之枢机，谈何容易？凡在众庶，一言不善，则人记之，成其耻累，况是万乘之主，不可出言有所乖失。其所亏损至大，岂同匹夫！我常以此为戒。隋炀帝初幸甘泉宫，泉石称意，而怪无萤火，敕云：'捉取萤火，于宫中照夜。'所司遽遣数千人采拾，送五百舆于宫侧，小事尚尔，况其大乎？"

魏徵对曰："人君居四海之尊，若有亏失，古人以为如日月之蚀，人皆见之，实如陛下所戒慎。"

In the eighth year of Right Done, Grandsire of T'ang said to his officials: "Words are a pivot for a gentleman. It's not an easy matter, is it? Even a wrong word uttered by an ordinary person can be remembered, and it can even be a shame or burden, let alone words from a sovereign of a great country. An emperor cannot afford a single wrong word, which may be a huge loss. So I take it as a lesson. Emperor Yang of Sui arrived at Sweet Spring Palace where rocks and springs pleased him. However, he complained about the lack of glowworms and ordered: "Catch some to light up the palace at night. Thousands of people were sent to catch glowworms, and five hundred carriages of glowworms were brought to the palace. A trifle can be like this, let alone big events". Cheng Wei replied: "A lord has a paramount position over all, a lapse of his, as held by ancients, is like solar or lunar eclipse, which can be seen by all. Your Majesty does need to be wary and cautious."

10. 悔过 Repentance

贞观二年，太宗谓房玄龄曰："为人大须学问。朕往为群凶未定，东西征讨，躬亲戎事，不暇读书。比来四海安静，身处殿堂，不能自执书卷，使人读而听之。君臣父子，政教之道，并在书内。古人云：'不学，墙面，莅事唯烦。'不徒言也。却思少小时行事，大觉非也。"

In the second year of Right Done, Grandsire of T'ang said to Hsuanling Fang: "A man needs to be learned. In my early days, I conquered far and near and led soldiers to fight tenacious enemies, so there was no time for me to read. In recent years, all under Heaven have been stabilized, so I, now in court, need to have someone read for me, as I can't sit to read. The ethics between lord and official, father and son, and knowledge of politics and cultivation are all in books. As ancients said, 'Not learned, one would go blank like facing a wall, and might fall if cornered'. It is no empty talk at all. Now I recall the things I did when young and realize many were wrong."

11. 崇儒学 Admiring Confucianism

贞观二年，太宗谓侍臣曰："为政之要，唯在得人。用非其才，必难致理。今所任用，必须以德行、学识为本。"

谏议大夫王珪曰："人臣若无学业，不能识前言往行，岂堪大任？"

The second year of Right Done found Grandsire of Tang tell his courtiers: "The key to governance lies in using proper talents, otherwise, it would be difficult to govern well. Nowadays, when using talents you should focus on their conduct and knowledge." Kuei Wang, the imperial censor, said: "How could officials undertake the responsibility if they have no knowledge and remember no words and deeds from the ancients?"

12. 务农 Agriculture

贞观二年，太宗谓侍臣曰："凡事皆须务本。国以人为本，人以衣食为本，凡营衣食，以不失时为本。夫不失时者，在人君简静乃可致耳。若兵戈屡动，土木不息，而欲不夺农时，其可得乎？"

王珪曰："昔秦皇、汉武，外则穷极兵戈，内则崇侈宫室，人力既竭，祸难遂兴。彼岂不欲安人乎？失所以安人之道也。亡隋之辙，殷鉴不远，陛下亲承其弊，知所以易之。然在初则易，终之实难。伏愿慎终如始，方尽其美。"

太宗曰："公言是也。夫安人宁国，惟在于君。君无为则人乐，君多欲则人苦。朕所以抑情损欲，克己自励耳。"

In the second year of Right Done, Grandsire of T'ang said to his officials: "Efforts must be directed to the base. A country is based on its people, and people on food and clothing. The cultivation of crops and mulberry trees is based on timing. To catch the timing, a sovereign should be quiet. How can he catch it with continuous fighting and endless building while expecting not to miss farming? Minister Kui Wang said: "In the past, Emperor First of Ch'in and Emperor Martial of Han launched battle after battle with other countries, while they indulged in luxury in the palace. Energy was exhausted, and disasters came as a result. Didn't they want to settle people? They just missed the right direction. I do hope Your Majesty can administrate affairs prudently all the time so as to have the best result". Grandsire of T'ang said: "You are quite right. The key to settlement lies in the lord. People will be joyful if a lord does nothing against Nature; people will be painful if a lord is full of desires. That is why I press down my desires and exhort myself to do better."

13. 征伐 Expedition

抚万姓以慈，遇群臣以礼。

A lord should treat people with kindness, and officials with rites.

第五节 《资治通鉴》
Section 5 *History as a Mirror*

1. 周纪一 The First Volume of the Records of Chough

夫才与德异，而世俗莫之能辨，通谓之贤，此其所以失人也。夫聪察强毅之谓才，正直中和之谓德。才者，德之资也；德者，才之帅也。……是故才德全尽谓之“圣人”，才德兼亡谓之“愚人”；德胜才谓之“君子”，才胜德谓之“小人”。

Talent differs from virtue. But the worldly cannot distinguish between the two and term both of them as virtuousness, which leads to the misjudgment of people. Talent is said to include wit, insight, strength and endurance while virtue is said to include fairness, uprightness, mediocrity and harmony. Talent supplements virtue, and virtue governs talent.…Therefore, a man of both virtue and talent is called a “saint” and a man without either called a “fool”; a man whose virtue is above talent is called a “gentleman” and a man whose talent is above virtue is called a “flunky”.

2. 周纪二 The Second Volume of the Records of Chough

夫信者，人君之大宝也。国保于民，民保于信；非信无以使民，非民无以守国。是故古之王者不欺四海，霸者不欺四邻，善为国者不欺其民，善为家者不欺其亲。不善者反之，欺其邻国，欺其百姓，甚者欺其兄弟，欺其父子。上不信下，下不信上，上下离心，以至于败。所利不能药其所伤，所获不能补其所亡，岂不哀哉！昔齐桓公不背曹沫之盟，晋文公不贪伐原之利，魏文侯不弃虞人之期，秦孝公不废徙木之赏。此四君者道非粹白，而商君尤称刻薄，又处战攻之世，天下趋于诈力，犹且不敢忘信以畜其民，况为四海治平之政者哉！

Faith is a treasure for rulers. A state is defended by its people and people defended by faith. Without faith, no people can be worked; without people, no state can be guarded. Therefore, of yore, rulers never cheated their people and overlords never bullied neighboring states and heads of households never bullied their relatives. On the contrary, now a bad ruler bullies his neighboring states, bullies his people, bullies fathers and sons and brothers. The ruler and his people don't trust each other and such a state will end up dying out. With the little advantage he's got by cheating, he cannot cure a fatal wound at all. What he gains is far less than what he loses. Isn't it distressing?! Then Lord Column of the State of Ch'i kept the Alliance imposed by Tsao Mo; Lord Civil of the State of Chin kept the promise without fighting for the land; Lord Civil of Way obeyed the appointment of hunting with the mountainous people; Lord Piety of Ch'in did not break the promise to the man who moved the pole. According to Lordson Yang's critical comments, though these four lords did not have perfect governance, and Shang Yang was extremely harsh, and they were engaged in battles and living in a world full of craft, they dared not forget faith to win people, not to mention the present rulers to pacify the world!

3. 周纪四 The Forth Volume of the Records of Chough

卫平侯薨，子嗣君立。卫有胥靡亡之魏，因为魏王之后治病。嗣君闻之，请以五十金买之。五反，魏不与，乃以左氏易之。左右谏曰："夫以一都买一胥靡，可乎？"嗣君曰："非子所知也！夫治无小，乱无大。法不立，诛不必，虽有十左氏，无益也。法立，诛必，失十左氏，无害也。"魏王闻之曰："人主之欲，不听之不祥。"因载而往，徒献之。

When Marquess Peace of Watch demised, his son Successor of Watch acceded to the throne. Then a convict escaped to Way for the treatment of Queen of Way's illness. When hearing that, the new crown demanded to buy him back for 50 taels of gold. After repeated negotiations, the State of Way still refused the deal. The lord intended to exchange the convict with the city of Tso. Courtiers nearby remonstrated: "Is a convict worth a city?" The lord replied, "It is what you don't understand! No trivial matters ignored, no disturbance arising. With no law established or death penalty executed, what's the use of ten cities like Tso?

With law established or death penalty executed, it will be quite harmless even if ten cities are lost." Hearing of that, the king of Way sighed, "If he is not satisfied, he will bring us trouble." Thus, he ordered to send the convict back in a cart without asking for remuneration.

4. 秦纪二 The Second Volume of the Records of Ch'in

夫为国家者，任官以才，立政以礼，怀民以仁，交邻以信；是以官得其人，政得其节，百姓怀其德，四邻亲其义。夫如是，则国家安如磐石。

Those who reign a state should employ talents as officials, administer affairs with rituals, reassure people with benevolence, and treat neighbors with credit, hence talents in office, rituals for administration, people feeling the virtue and neighbors trusting the credit. In this case, the state will be as solid as a rock.

5. 汉纪三 The Third Volume of the Records of Han

创业垂统之君，躬行节俭以示子孙，其末流犹入于淫靡，况示之以侈乎！

Monarchs who founded their nation and left it to their heirs always exerted frugality and set them a good example. In due time, their heirs would indulge in excesses themselves, let alone shown the extravagance?

6. 汉纪九 The Ninth Volume of the Records of Han

渐民以仁，摩民以谊，节民以礼，故其刑罚甚轻而禁不犯者，教化行而习俗美也。

Rulers should edify people with kindness, encourage people with righteousness, moderate people with rites, therefore, even though punishments are light, people won't disobey. As cultivation goes, customs improve.

为治者不至多言，顾力行何如耳！

A ruler should not talk too much; he should consider if he can do well.

7. 汉纪十 The Tenth Volume of the Records of Han

善恶要于功罪而不淫于毁誉，听其言而责其事，举其名而指其实。

The essence of identifying one lies in his merits or sins rather than slanders or compliments. It requires facts as the antithesis on hearing some rumors, and actual merits to verify him on hearing a recommendation.

8. 汉纪十一 The Eleventh Volume of the Records of Han

上招延士大夫，常如不足；然性严峻，群臣虽素所爱信者，或小有犯法，或欺罔，辄按诛之，无所宽假。汲黯谏曰："陛下求贤甚劳，未尽其用，辄已杀之。以有限之士恣无已之诛，臣恐天下贤才将尽，陛下谁与共为治乎！"黯言之甚怒，上笑而谕之曰："何世无才，患人不能识之耳。苟能识之，何患无人！夫所谓才者，犹有用之器也，有才而不肯尽用，与无才同，不杀何施！"黯曰："臣虽不能以言屈陛下，而心犹以为非；愿陛下自今改之，无以臣为愚而不知理也。"上顾群臣曰："黯自言为便辟则不可，自言为愚，岂不信然乎！"

Lord Marshal of Han recruited scholars, as if always in fear of a shortage, but he was strict and harsh. Those who offended or deceived were sentenced to death according to law without forgiveness, be they faithful officials or not. Chi'an remonstrated: "Your Majesty has tried hard to recruit talents, but they are killed before playing their role. Considering the limited number of scholars and your unlimited sentence, I am afraid all talents under Heaven will be killed, and then with whom will Your Majesty manage the state?" So saying, he was raged, but Lord Marshal of Han laughed to explain: "Aren't there talents? They are not yet found. If one can find them, why does he have to worry? 'Talent' is just a useful gear. Talents not working well are but non-talents, then why should I hesitate to kill them?" Chi'an said: "I can't persuade Your Majesty with words, but I still don't think that is right. I hope Your Majesty would change from now, and do not think I am ignorant and unreasonable." Lord Marshal of Han turned to the officials around: "If Chi'an is held as flattering, that is not true. But we can say he's ignorant, can't we?"

9. 汉纪十六 The Sixteenth Volume of the Records of Han

夫广厦之下，细旃之上，明师居前，劝诵在后，上论唐、虞之际，下及殷、周之盛，考仁圣之风，习治国之道，欣欣焉发愤忘食，日新厥德，其乐岂衔橛之间哉！

In a commodious hall, on a soft blanket, and under the guidance of a good teacher, I recite and read classics, discussing the heyday of Mound and Hibiscus to the prosperity of Shang and Chough, looking into the manner of sublime sovereigns, and learning the way to administrate a state, which is a great joy to me. I indulge in this joy so much so that I even forget eating, finding my virtue enhanced everyday. Would I gain the same joy on horseback?

10. 汉纪十七 The Seventeenth Volume of the Records of Han

贤而多财，则损其志；愚而多财，则益其过。

Much property erodes a worthy's will, and increases a fool's folly.

11. 汉纪二十一 The Twenty-First Volume of the Records of the Han Dynasty

故德必核其真，然后授其位；能必核其真，然后授其事；功必核其真，然后授其赏；罪必核其真，然后授其刑；行必核其真，然后贵之；言必核其真，然后信之。

One's virtue must be verified before appointment; one's ability must be verified before employment; one's merit must be verified before awarding; one's sin must be verified before punishment; one's good deed must be verified before praising; one's remarks must be verified before trusting.

12. 汉纪二十四 The Twenty-Forth Volume of the Records of Han

下有其萌，然后变见于上，可不致慎！祸起细微，奸生所易。

Misfortune shows up where a bane germinates, so how could one not be prudent? A calamity comes from where it is unseen, and evil arises out of negligence.

13. 汉纪四十三 The Forty-Third Volume of the Records of Han

道德足以尊主，智能足以庇民，被褐怀玉，深藏不市。

Morality upholds the lord; talent protects the folk. Real treasures are hidden in one's clothes, not for sale.

取其道不取其人，务其实不务其名。

Appoint talents according to their virtue, based on their deeds rather than their name.

14. 高祖武皇帝十五 Record of Lord Marshal, Highroot of Liang

上为人孝慈恭俭，博学能文，阴阳、卜筮、骑射、声律、草隶、围棋，无不精妙。勤于政务，冬月四更竟，即起视事，执笔触寒，手为皴裂。自天监中用释氏法，长斋断鱼肉，日止一食，唯菜羹、粝饭而已，或遇事繁，日移中则嗽口以过。身衣布衣，木绵皂帐，一冠三载，一衾二年，后宫贵妃以下，衣不曳地。性不饮酒，非宗庙祭祀、大飨宴及诸法事，未尝作乐。虽居暗室，恒理衣冠，小坐、盛暑，未尝褰袒。

The lord was filial and kind, polite and frugal, erudite and capable, who was good at writing, Shade and Shine, divination, riding and shooting, prosody, cursive calligraphy and go playing. He was hardworking in state affairs. Right after three o'clock at winter dawn, he got up to work. Due to the severe coldness, his hand got chapped, having held a brush pen for so long. Since the days of Tienchien when he converted to Buddhism, he had been abstaining from meat and fish, only one simple coarse meal a day. Sometimes, having so much work, and the sun having moved overhead, he only gargled to count it as a meal. He wore sack clothes and used a black cotton mosquito net. A hat he would use for three years and a quilt he would change in two years. His imperial concubines who ranked below the highest could not wear a maxiskirt. Apart from that, he didn't drink wine by nature, he wouldn't give order to play music except at a fete in a shrine or a grand banquet or Buddha-worshiping activities. Although in a dim room, he was neatly dressed, never topless, even in the hottest summer.

15. 唐纪二 The Second Volume of the Records of T'ang

丈夫一言许人，千金不易。

A man's promise no bars of gold can buy.

16. 唐纪八 The Eighth Volume of the Records of T'ang

君依于国，国依于民。刻民以奉君，犹割肉以充腹，腹饱而身毙，君富而国亡。故人君之患，不自外来，常由身出。夫欲盛则费广，费广则赋重，赋重则民愁，民愁则国危，国危则君丧矣。

A lord depends on the state, and the state on people. Exploitation of people for the lord's greed is like cutting flesh to satisfy the belly; the belly is full but the body is dead; the lord is rich but the state is finished. Therefore, a lord's disaster comes not from outside but from himself. The more a lord's greed is, the more he spends; the more he spends, the more taxes he levies; the more taxes he levies, the more people worry; the more people worry, the more risky the state is;

the more risky the country is, the sooner the lord loses his power and dies.

兼听则明，偏信则暗。

Harking to both, you are enlightened; heeding but one, you are beclouded.

夫国以法理，军以法胜；有恩无威，慈母不能使其子。陛下厚养战士而每战少，岂非无法邪！……王法有无，国家乃为之轻重。

A country runs with law and an army wins with law. With love but no discipline, a loving mother cannot manage her son well. Your Majesty treats soldiers well but they rarely win a war. Isn't it because of no law? … Thus, whether there is law or not is a basic premise on which a country exists.

17. 唐纪十 The Tenth Volume of the Records of T'ang

为官择人，不可造次。用一君子，则君子皆至；用一小人，则小人竞进矣。

Do not make a hasty decision on the appointment of officials. As a gentleman is appointed, other gentlemen will come; once a flunky is appointed, the same kind spring up.

18. 唐纪五十 The Fiftieth Volume of the Records of T'ang

夫地力之生物有大限，取之有度，用之有节，则常足。取之无度，用之无节，则常不足。生物之丰败由天，用物之多少由人，是以圣王立程，量入为出，虽遇灾难，下无困穷。理化既衰，则乃反是，量出为入，不恤所无。桀用天下而不足，汤用七十里而有馀，是乃用之盈虚在节与不节耳。

There is a limit to growth. Therefore, one can be rich if he takes within a limit and spends with moderation, or he will be short of supplies if he squanders. It is Heaven that decides productivity, but it is man that decides consumption. For that consideration, wise kings will issue regulations to measure proceeds for expenditure, so his people won't suffer from shortages in case of a catastrophe.

Oppositely, when politics and cultivation fail, proceeds won't be considered for expenditure. Stump didn't feel having enough even though he exhausted the world, but Hotspring of Shang still had surplus though he could only gain products from a land of 35 square kilometers, as indicates that whether there is surplus or not is a matter of moderation.

第三章　经学
Chapter Ⅲ　Confucian Classics

第一节　《周易》
Section 1　*Changes*

1. 系辞 Attribution

古者包牺氏之王天下也，仰则观象于天，俯则观法于地，观鸟兽之文，与地之宜，近取诸身，远取诸物，于是始作八卦，以通神明之德，以类万物之情。

Of yore, when Hidden Spirit ruled the world, he looked up to signs in the sky, overlooked changes on land, watched traces of birds and animals and their relations with the environment, and created Eight Diagrams with reference to his body and the things far away so as to communicate with sages for truth and illustrate the nature of all things.

形而上者谓之道，形而下者谓之器。

What is high above is the Word; what is down below is the vessel.

是故《易》有太极，是生两仪，两仪生四象，四象生八卦，八卦定吉凶，吉凶生大业。

Change has its Great Ultimate, which begets Two Sides, which in turn beget Four Icons, which in turn beget Eight Symbols. Eight Symbols determine good luck and bad luck, which in turn engender great causes.

备物致用，立功成器，以为天下利，莫大乎圣人。

No one can surpass a saint, who prepares things for use, as tools to facilitate the world.

天尊地卑，乾坤定矣。卑高以陈，贵贱位矣。动静有常，刚柔断矣。方以类聚，物以群分，吉凶生矣。在天成象，在地成形，变化见矣。是故刚柔相摩，八卦相荡。鼓之以雷霆，润之以风雨；日月运行，一寒一暑。乾道成男，坤道成女。乾知大始，坤作成物。乾以易知，坤以简能。易则易知，简则易从。易知则有亲，易从则有功。有亲则可久，有功则可大。可久则贤人之德，可大则贤人之业。易简而天下之理得。天下之理得而成位乎其中矣。

Heaven is high and earth low, hence the order of Gen and Kueen. Lowness and highness are placed in order, hence the status of peers and commons; motion and stillness obey a rule, hence the determination of robustness and frailty; people or things gather according to their kinds, hence the emergence of auspices and banes. With icons in Heaven and forms on earth, changes take place. Therefore, rigidity and fluidity scrape each other and eight diagrams swing to each other. Moved with thunder and lightning, moistened with wind and rain, the sun and moon cycle from cold to heat, so males come into being in accordance with Gen and females in accordance with Kueen. Gen knows the beginning and Kueen rears all; Gen reveals wisdom with ease, and Kueen displays functions with brevity. With ease, it's easy to be known; with brevity, it's easy to follow. Easy to be known, it's accessible; easy to follow, it's successful. Accessible, it lasts long; successful, it develops well. Lasting long, a sage has great virtues; developing well, a sage has great merits. Understanding ease and brevity, you know what it is between Heaven and earth; knowing what it is between Heaven and earth, you have all successes waiting for you.

一阴一阳之谓道，继之者善也，成之者性也。仁者见之谓之仁，知者见之谓之知，百姓日用而不知，故君子之道鲜矣。显诸仁，藏诸用，鼓万物而不与圣人同忧，盛德大业至矣哉！富有之谓大业，日新之谓盛德。生生之谓易，成象之谓乾，效法之谓坤，极数知来之谓占，通变之谓事，阴阳不测之谓神。

What is called Shade and Shine is the Word. What follows it is Good; what makes it is Nature. He who is benevolent calls it Benevolence; he who is wise calls it Wisdom. The folks use it but don't know it, so very few talk about it. The benevolence of the Word is revealed; the use of the Word is hidden. It raises everything without saints' worries, hence the completion of great virtues and causes! Gaining wealth is called Great Cause; making progress is called Great Virtue. Making lives live on is called Change; visualizing things is called Gen; sustaining things is called Kueen; calculating to predict is called Divination; access to the secrets of change is called Acumen; not knowing the reason of Shade and Shine is called Mystery.

与天地相似，故不违。知周乎万物而道济天下，故不过。旁行而不流，乐天知命，故不忧。安土敦乎仁，故能爱。范围天地之化而不过，曲成万物而不遗，通乎昼夜之道而知，故神无方而《易》无体。

Change is similar to Heaven and earth, so it has no obstructions. Its wisdom spreads to all and its Word benefits everything, so it has no rivals. It runs together with Heaven and earth, never astray. It is settled to be benevolent, hence full of love. All the changes between Heaven and earth are included, and nothing created is lost, and the cycling of day and night is well understood, therefore Heaven has bounds and *Changes* has no form.

二人同心，其利断金。同心之言，其臭如兰。

The same mind if two hold, it can cut gold; the same mind can speak well, a balmy smell.

天之所助者顺也，人之所助者信也。履信思乎顺，又以尚贤也。是以“自天佑之，吉无不利”也。

Heaven helps him who follows the Word; people help him who has good credit. As he has credit, follows the Word and worships sages, he has help from Heaven. He is lucky, and there is nothing unfavorable.

君子上交不谄，不交不渎。

A gentleman won't flatter his superiors, and won't look down upon his inferiors.

子曰："乾坤，其《易》之门邪？乾，阳物也；坤，阴物也。阴阳合德而刚柔有体，以体天地之撰，以通神明之德。其称名也，杂而不越，于稽其类，其衰世之意邪？"夫《易》，彰往而察来，而微显阐幽。开而当名，辨物，正言，断辞，则备矣。其称名也小，其取类也大；其旨远，其辞文；其言曲而中，其事肆而隐。因贰以济民行，以明失得之报。

Confucius said: "Aren't Gen and Kueen two doors to *Change*?" Gen is Shine, and Kueen Shade. The virtuous mating of Shine and Shade makes things properly hard or soft to reveal the writings of Heaven and earth and to reach the virtue of divinity. Though names are various, there are no transgressions. Doesn't an examination of their kinds show symbols in declining order?" *Change* illuminates the past, predicts the future and illustrates what is tiny and hidden. Open it, and we see proper names that distinguish all things, make sound judgments and correct predictions, so perfect! The names though little refer to large kinds and expresses great purports elegantly; the words, though insinuative, hit the target; the things, though expressed, are obscure. It serves the people in forms of auxiliaries and enlightens the retribution of losses and gains.

2. 乾卦第一 Diagram 1: Gen

天行，健。君子以自强不息。

Heaven goes it strong, and a gentleman strive on.

九二：见龙在田，利见大人。

Shine the Second: A dragon in the field, it is good to meet a lord.

九三：君子终日乾乾，夕惕若厉，无咎。

Shine the Third: A gentleman is careful all day long, vigilant even at sunset, hence no errors.

利者，义之和也。

Profit is the result of righteousness.

夫大人者，与天地合其德，与日月合其明，与四时合其序，与鬼神合其吉凶。先天下而天弗违，后天而奉天时。天且弗违，而况于人乎！况于鬼神乎！

A great Lord has his virtues in harmony with Heaven and earth, has his brightness in harmony with the sun and the moon, has his order in harmony with the four seasons, and has his auspices and omens in harmony with ghosts and gods. He acts before Heaven, but Heaven does not blame him; he acts after Heaven and follows the rhythm of Heaven. Heaven does not blame him, let alone men, let alone ghosts.

3．坤卦第二 Diagram 2: Kueen

地势，坤，君子以厚德载物。

The earth rears all, and a gentleman raises things with virtue.

4．需卦第五 Diagram 5: Need

需，须也。险在前也，刚健而不陷，其义不困穷矣。

The hexagram Need means necessity. Facing a danger, he is strong and sound, without panicking, and by appearance, not anxious.

5．泰卦第十一 Diagram 11: Tower

九三：无平不陂，无往不复。

Shine the Third: No slope, no level road; no going, no return.

6. 否卦第十二 Diagram 12: Obstacle

君子以俭德辟难，不可荣以禄。

A gentleman avoid dangers with thrift, and does not pursue honors and riches.

7. 剥卦第二十三 Diagram 23: Spall

君子尚消息盈虚，天行也。

A gentleman pays attention to the rise and fall, surplus and vacuity of Shade and Shine, as is the Word of Heaven.

8. 颐卦第二十七 Diagram 27: Ease

六四：虎视眈眈，其欲逐逐。

Shade the Fourth: A tiger fixing its eyes has its desire greatly rise.

9. 明夷卦第三十六 Diagram 36: Archery

初九：明夷于飞垂其翼。君子于行，三日不食。

Shine the First: Wings lowered, the pheasant flies; three days, he's no supplies.

10. 损卦第四十一 Diagram 41: Wane

六三：三人行则损一人；一人行则得其友。

Shade the Third: In a company of three, one will harmed be; when alone one does wend, he'll find his friend.

11. 震卦第五十一 Diagram 51: Thunder

震来虩虩，笑言哑哑。震惊百里，不丧匕鬯。

At thunders one shudders; free of guile, many smile. Thunder rumbles far way; as usual, rituals stay.

12. 艮卦第五十二 Diagram 52: Choke

六五：艮其辅，言有序，悔亡。

Shade the Fifth: Close the mouth and speak logically to avoid errors.

13. 丰卦第五十五 Diagram 55: Harvest

日中则昃，月盈则食，天地盈虚，与时消息，而况于人乎！况于鬼神乎！

The sun rises high to skew, and the moon waxes to wane. Everything varies according to time between Heaven and earth, let alone men, let alone those demons and spirits.

14. 中孚卦第六十一 Diagram 61: Integrity

九二：鸣鹤在阴，其子和之。我有好爵，吾与尔靡之。

Shine the Second: A crane sings in the shade; its child follows the sound. I have a jar of jade; let's pass the wind around!

15. 序卦 Order

有天地然后有万物，有万物然后有男女，有男女然后有夫妇，有夫妇然后有父子，有父子然后有君臣，有君臣然后有上下，有上下然后礼义有所错。

Heaven and earth existed before all things on earth; all things existed before men and women; men and women existed before husbands and wives, husbands and wives existed before fathers and sons; fathers and sons existed before lords and subjects; lords and subjects existed before superiors and inferiors; superiors and inferiors existed before the handling of laws, rites and morality.

第二节 《尚书》
Section 2 *High Book*

1. 尧典 Record of Lord Mound

曰若稽古，帝尧曰放勋。钦明文思安安，允恭克让，光被四表，格于上下。克明俊德，以亲九族。九族既睦，平章百姓。百姓昭明，协和万邦。黎民于变时雍。

乃命羲和，钦若昊天，历象日月星辰，敬授民时。分命羲仲，宅嵎夷，曰旸谷。寅宾出日，平秩东作。日中，星鸟，以殷仲春。厥民析，鸟兽孳尾。申命羲叔，宅南交，曰明都。平秩南讹，敬致。日永，星火，以正仲夏。厥民因，鸟兽希革。分命和仲，宅西，曰昧谷。寅饯纳日，平秩西成。宵中，星虚，以殷仲秋。厥民夷，鸟兽毛毨。申命和叔，宅朔方，曰幽都。平在朔易。日短，星昴，以正仲冬。厥民隩，鸟兽鹬毛。

帝曰："咨！汝羲暨和。期三百有六旬有六日，以闰月定四时，成岁。允厘百工，庶绩咸熙。"

In antiquity, Lord Mound, dubbed Free Merit (Fanghsun), was respectful, perspicacious, orderly, thoughtful and benign. His sincerity and responsibility shone everywhere between Heaven and earth. He praised virtue to harmonize his kinsmen; kinsmen harmonized, he discerned and promoted officials; officials properly managed, he coordinated all vassals, therefore people everywhere became friendly and harmonious.

He ordered She-Her to do everything in deference to divine law, including making a calendar in accordance with the movement of the sun, the moon and the stars and educating people to live and work in deference on a nature-dependent basis. Here is how he gave them specific orders. The second son of She was ordered to live at Sunrise Valley (Yangku, the East End) to welcome the sunrise in absolute respect while observing the movement of the sun. Hence Spring Equinox is the day on which the day and night are of the same length, and Prime of Spring is the day on which the Bird appears right in the middle of the southern sky. This is the time when people work in fields, and fowls and herds begin to mate. The third son of She was ordered to live at Crosstoes (Chiaochih, the South End) to wait for the sun in absolute respect and to watch its southbound course. Hence Summer Solstice is the day with the longest daytime, and Prime of Summer is the day on which the Fire appears right in the middle of the southern sky. This is the time when people choose to live at a higher place, and birds' feathers and animal furs begin to shed. The second son of Her (Hochung) was ordered to live at Sunset Valley (Meiku, the West End) to see the sun off in absolute respect, to record about the sunset and to decide on matters of autumn harvest." This is the time when people go back to live at a lower place, and fowls and herds put on new feathers or furs. The third son of Her (Hoshu) was ordered to live at Chillton (Dim Town, the North End) to watch the sun's northbound course. Hence Winter Solstice is the day with the shortest daytime, and Prime of Winter is the day on which the Mao appears right in the middle of the southern sky. This is the time when people choose to live indoors, and fowls and herds begin to grow their fuzz.

Mound remarked: "Ah, you members of She-Her, I hope you can set the cycle at 366 days, and set the seasons with the help of a leap month, and a year is thus set. then all the officials will know their duties and everything will work accordingly."

月正元日，舜格于文祖，询于四岳，辟四门，明四目，达四聪。咨十有二牧，曰："食哉惟时！柔远能迩，惇德允元，而难任人，蛮夷率服。"

舜曰："咨！四岳。有能奋庸熙帝之载，使宅百揆，亮采惠畴？"佥曰："伯禹作司空。"帝曰："俞！咨禹，汝平水土，惟时懋哉！"禹拜稽首，让于稷、契暨皋陶。帝曰："俞，汝往哉！"

帝曰："弃，黎民阻饥，汝后稷，播时百谷。"

帝曰："契！百姓不亲，五品不逊。汝作司徒，敬敷五教，在宽。"

帝曰："皋陶！蛮夷猾夏，寇贼奸宄。汝作士，五刑有服，五服三就。五流有宅，五宅三居。惟明克允。"

帝曰："畴若予工？"佥曰："垂哉！"帝曰："俞！咨垂，汝共工。"垂拜稽首，让于殳、斨暨伯与。帝曰："俞！往哉，汝谐。"

帝曰："畴若予上下草木鸟兽？"佥曰："益哉！"帝曰："俞！咨益，汝作朕虞。"益拜稽首，让于朱虎熊罴。帝曰："俞！往哉，汝谐。"

帝曰："咨！四岳。有能典朕三礼？"佥曰："伯夷。"帝曰："俞！咨伯。汝作秩宗。夙夜惟寅，直哉惟清。"伯拜稽首，让于夔、龙。帝曰："俞，往，钦哉！"

帝曰："夔！命汝典乐，教胄子。直而温，宽而栗，刚而无虐，简而无傲。诗言志，歌永言，声依永，律和声。八音克谐，无相夺伦，神人以和。"夔曰："於！予击石拊石，百兽率舞。"

帝曰："龙！朕堲谗说殄行，震惊联师。命汝作纳言，夙夜出纳朕命，惟允。"

帝曰："咨！汝二十有二人，钦哉！惟时亮天功。"

The first day of First Moon, Hibiscus paid a visit to Mound's Temple and there discussed with vassal lords from all directions. The four gates were opened so that everyone could see and hear clearly. He said to lords of twelve states: "Food must be produced in time! If we pacify those distant and love those near, be friendly to virtuous ones, trust the good, and reject the evil, aliens and barbarians will obey. "

"Ah!" said Lord Hibiscus, "Lords of all states! Who can endeavor to prosper the cause of Lord Mound and be a prime minister to assist me with national affairs?"

All replied: "Lord Worm is Grand Builder." Hibiscus said: "Ah! Good. Worm, you did a good job in controlling flood! Now try your best." Worm bowed and would offer the post to Corn, Deal and Moor Potter.

Lord Hibiscus said, "Well, Worm, you go ahead."

And Lord Hibiscus said to Abandon, "Now people are starving, you can take charge of farming, sowing all grains!"

And Hibiscus turned to Deal: "Now the folks do not love each other, the families are not harmonious. Deal, you can manage civil affairs and carefully carry out the education of five constants. Try to be lenient."

Hibiscus said to Moor Potter, "The barbarians are invading our land, evildoers within and without. You can be a justice. There are various methods for the five penalties to be used in the countryside, in towns and at court. And there are various places for the five kinds of exile, in three different distances. You should judge impartially!"

And Lord Hibiscus asked, "Who can take charge of the hundred trades?"

All replied: "Droop!"

Hibiscus said, "All right! Droop, you take charge of the trades." Droop bowed his thanks and would transfer the offer to Long Axe and First Giver.

Hibiscus said, "All right. You go ahead with them."

Hibiscus asked: "Who will take charge of plants and animals in hills and swamps?"

All replied: "More can do that!"

Hibiscus said, "That's good. More, you can take the job."

More bowed his thanks and would transfer the offer to Scarlet, Tiger, Bear and Bruin.

Hibiscus said, "All right, you go together."

Hibiscus said: "Ah! Lords of all states, who can preside over the three sacrifices?"

All replied: "Lord Bow."

Hibiscus said: "All right, Bow, you take care of sacrifices. Be respectful from morning to evening, be just and sagacious."

Lord Bow bowed his thanks and would transfer the offer to One Leg Monster and Dragon.

And Hibiscus said, "All right, go ahead, do take care."

Hibiscus said: "One Leg Monster! I'd like to appoint you as a music officer. Teach the young and be honest and gentle, generous and firm, strong and but not rude, simple but not arrogant. Poetry is to express the will, singing is speaking. Notes are based on singing, and tunes attune them. The notes of the eight musical instruments can be mediated so that they don't mess, then God and people will be harmonious."

One Leg Monster said: "Ah! I will beat the stone chime to make those playing animals dance."

Hibiscus said: "Dragon! I'm disgusted at slander and corruption, which will shock my people. I appoint you as an official of information, convey my order early and late, and pass me public opinion. It must be true!"

Hibiscus said: "Ah! 22 of you! Do take care. You should be good leaders."

2. 洪范 Universal Norms

无偏无陂，遵王之义；无有作好，遵王之道；无有作恶，遵王之路。

No bias or partiality, but respect for righteousness of the King; no favoritism, but respect for the Word of the King; no misconduct, but respect for the ways of the King.

惟十有三祀，王访于箕子。王乃言曰："呜呼！箕子，惟天阴骘下民，相协厥居，我不知其彝伦攸叙。"

箕子乃言曰："我闻在昔鲧陻洪水，汩陈其五行。帝乃震怒，不畀洪范九畴，彝伦攸斁。鲧则殛死，禹乃嗣兴。天乃锡禹洪范九畴，彝伦攸叙。初一曰五行，次二曰敬用五事，次三曰农用八政，次四曰协用五纪，次五曰建用皇极，次六曰乂用三德，次七曰明用稽疑，次八曰念用庶征，次九曰向用五福，威用六极。"

In the 13th year of King Civil, King Martial paid a visit to Sir Winnow to make an inquiry, "Ah, Sir Winnow, Heaven blessed his subjects with harmony, and I wonder what Heaven's law is."

Sir Winnow replied, "I hear in the olden days when Big Fish hampered the flow of flood, confused Five Elements and offended God, God did not give him the law to govern, hence a great disturbance. Then Worm rose when Big Fish died in exile. God granted Worm the laws to govern. First, follow the order of Five Elements; second, mind looks and senses in deference; third, fulfil eight administrative affairs; fourth, use five timing methods properly; fifth, establish the supreme principle; sixth, manage the people with three virtues; seventh, respond to questioning in a clear manner; eighth, study omens carefully; ninth, advise the people with five fortunes and establish authority by means of six disciplines."

3. 皋陶谟 Moor Potter's Counsel

曰若稽古，皋陶曰："允迪厥德，谟明弼谐。"

Moor Potter consulted the old files, saying:"Fulfilling his duty with virtue, a lord will be foresighted, and his ministers will help him."

禹曰："俞！如何？"

Worm asked: "Yes, how?"

皋陶曰："都！慎厥身，修思永。惇叙九族，庶明励翼，迩可远在兹。"

Moor Potter replied: "Yeah, he must cultivate himself with prudence and think afar. Making his kin tolerant and obedient and sages helpful to him, he should start at hand and then appease those afar."

禹拜昌言曰："俞。"

Worm bowed to Moor Potter and beamed: "Yes!"

皋陶曰："都！在知人，在安民。"

Moor Potter added: "Yeah, he should be able to judge, and settle people."

禹曰："吁！咸若时，惟帝其难之。知人则哲，能官人。安民则惠，黎民怀之。能哲而惠，何忧乎驩兜？何迁乎有苗？何畏乎巧言令色孔壬？"

Worm answered: “Oh, even Lord Hibiscus could not do both. He is wise who can judge, hence able to use people properly; he is kind who can settle people, and people will respect him. As he is wise and kind, why need he worry about Glee Helmet (Huant’ou)? Why need he exile Sprouts (Miaos)? Why need he fear the glib tongues and fawning looks of Deep Craft (Kungjen)?

皋陶曰：“都！亦行有九德。亦言其人有德，乃言曰：载采采。”

Moor Potter said: “Yeah, there are nine virtues to judge by. If one is virtuous, his virtues can be listed one by one.”

禹曰：“何？”

Worm asked: “What are they?”

皋陶曰：“宽而栗，柔而立，愿而恭，乱而敬，扰而毅，直而温，简而廉，刚而塞，强而义。彰厥有常吉哉！日宣三德，夙夜浚明有家。日严祗敬六德，亮采有邦。翕受敷施，九德咸事，俊乂在官。百僚师师，百工惟时，抚于五辰，庶绩其凝。无教逸欲有邦。兢兢业业，一日二日万几。无旷庶官，天工，人其代之。天叙有典，敕我五典五惇哉！天秩有礼，自我五礼有庸哉！同寅协恭和衷哉！天命有德，五服五章哉！天讨有罪，五刑五用哉！政事懋哉！懋哉！”

Moor Potter replied: “Tolerant with seriousness, gentle with independence, strict with courtesy, versatile with prudence, flexible with perseverance, righteous with friendliness, frank with principles, firm with strength, brave with kindness. People with these virtues should be praised. A senior official can keep his fief if he performs three of the nine each day and works hard with courtesy; a vassal lord can keep his state if he performs six of the nine in assisting state affairs. Officials should learn the virtues and follow suit. Everyone must fulfill his own duty so that political affairs follow the movements of Heaven. Everything can be done successfully. State officials should not indulge in comfort or lust. On the other hand, they should work very hard, for things change at every moment. Do not set empty positions. Work arranged by God must be done by people. God has set rules for interpersonal relationship. Fathers must be moral, mothers kind, elder brothers friendly, younger brothers courteous, and children filial. All these must be reinforced. God has set up a classification of inferiority and superiority. Lords and subjects must respect one another and get along well. God has assigned tasks to the virtuous and used five kinds of attires to reward them and five means of penalties for evils. All try hard, the state will prosper, will prosper!

4. 牧誓 A Pledge at Muyeh

王曰："古人有言曰：'牝鸡无晨；牝鸡之晨，惟家之索。'今商王受，惟妇言是用，昏弃厥肆祀，弗答；昏弃厥遗王父母弟，不迪；乃惟四方之多罪逋逃，是崇是长，是信是使，是以为大夫卿士，俾暴虐于百姓，以奸宄于商邑。今予发，惟恭行天之罚。"

King Martial said, "As is said, 'no hen crows at dawn; if she does, the household is doomed.' King Chow of Shang listens but to a woman now, neglecting ancestral sacrifices, despising his remanent brothers and cousins while respecting and trusting, employing and promoting vicious refugees, whom he appoints as archons and ministers. He maltreats the folk brutally and commits sins and felonies in Shang's capital. Now, upon Heaven's Mandate, I declare an expedition.

5. 商书·仲虺之诰 Book of Shang: Lizard's Admonition

能自得师者王，谓人莫己若者亡。好问则裕，自用则小。

He who learns from others reigns; he who regards himself better than others fails. He who asks for advice is rich; he who is self-righteous is small.

6. 盘庚 Pankeng

先王有服，恪谨天命。

Our former kings obeyed Heaven, as we should follow with great care.

明听朕言，无荒失朕命。呜呼！古我先后，罔不惟民之承。保后胥戚，鲜以不浮于天时。殷降大虐，先王不怀厥攸作，视民利用迁。汝曷弗念我古后之闻？承汝俾汝，惟喜康共，非汝有咎比于罚。予若吁怀兹新邑，亦惟汝故，以丕从厥志。今予将试以汝迁，安定厥邦。汝不忧朕心之攸困，乃咸大不宣乃心，钦念以忱，动予一人。尔惟自鞠自苦，若乘舟，汝弗济，臭厥载。尔忱不属，惟胥以沉。不其或稽，自怒曷瘳？汝不谋长以思乃灾，汝诞劝忧。今其有今罔后，汝何生在上？

Listen to me and do not neglect what I say. Oh, none of my forefathers failed to settle his people. As lord and subjects had a sense of crisis, they avoided disasters. Whenever a disaster befell, my forefathers, not content with their achievements, would prioritize and relocate their people. Why don't you do likewise? I accommodate to you and do as you wish because I want to ensure you all well-being, rather than punishing you for your wrongdoings. This is also why I pledge to you to stay assured about our prospect in the new capital. Now I'll lead you to safeguard our kingdom. You don't understand the challenges I face and you won't confide to me what you really want, but I've got so many ardent thoughts yet I'm all on my own. You are destroying yourself, just like staying in your boat to sink. You'd rather not pull together, you'll all sink. What good will it do if you are just angry without trying to find the causes? You advise me not to worry, but you don't make long-term plans or take measures. How can you live in this world without thinking about tomorrow?

7. 周书·泰誓 Book of Chough: Grand Pledge

惟天地万物父母，惟人万物之灵。

Heaven and Earth are the parents of all, and humans the spirits of all.

8. 周书·周官 Book of Chough: Officials of Chough

惟克果断，乃罔后艰。

Decisiveness nullifies difficulties.

9. 五子之歌 Songs of Five Lords

皇祖有训，民可近，不可下，民惟邦本，本固邦宁。

As our Sire taught, we should approach our people, not downplaying them, as they are the foundation of a nation, on which we are settled.

10. 康诰 Admonition to K’ang

王曰："呜呼！封，汝念哉！今民将在祇遹乃文考，绍闻衣德言。往敷求于殷先哲王，用保乂民。汝丕远惟商耇成人，宅心知训。别求闻由古先哲王，用康保民。弘于天，若德裕乃身，不废在王命。"

王曰："呜呼！小子封，恫瘝乃身，敬哉！天畏棐忱，民情大可见。小人难保，往尽乃心，无康好逸豫，乃其乂民。我闻曰：'怨不在大，亦不在小。'惠不惠，懋不懋。已！汝惟小子，乃服惟弘，王应保殷民，亦惟助王宅天命，作新民。"

王曰："呜呼！封，敬明乃罚。人有小罪，非眚，乃惟终，自作不典，式尔，有厥罪小，乃不可不杀。乃有大罪，非终，乃惟眚灾，适尔，既道极厥辜，时乃不可杀。"

王曰："呜呼！封，有叙时，乃大明服，惟民其敕懋和。若有疾，惟民其毕弃咎。若保赤子，惟民其康乂。非汝封刑人杀人，无或刑人杀人。非汝封又曰劓刵人，无或劓刵人。"

王曰："封，爽惟民迪吉康。我时其惟殷先哲王德，用康乂民作求。矧今民罔迪不适，不迪则罔政在厥邦。"

王曰："呜呼！封，敬哉！无作怨，勿用非谋非彝，蔽时忱。丕则敏德，用康乃心，顾乃德。远乃猷裕，乃以民宁，不汝瑕殄。"

The Lord said, "Ah, feoffee, remember this. Our subjects are following our father’s way in deference, so you should govern in accordance with his virtue. When you arrive in Yin far there, you should follow the way of their wise kings to govern, and think what the fogies think and know how to tame them. In addition, you should know how the previous sage kings governed to ensure their people's well-being. If your rule prevails like Heaven, the mission our late Lord passed down to us won't end in nothing."

The Lord said, "Ah, my young feoffee, be deferential and prudent, and prepare for sufferings. Do take care. Heaven help those who are honest, as can be seen from the folks. Menial folks are hard to govern. Do your utmost. Indolence won't give you good days and only the opposite can lead to good rule. I hear that it doesn't matter how much or little people may complain, so long as you can tame the untamed and develop the undeveloped. Young as you are, you'll be entrusted with great responsibilities. Now established, we should help to govern Yin with Heaven's Mandate, and upon Heaven's Mandate, you should continue to reform the people."

The Lord said, "Ah, feoffee, you must be careful with jurisdiction. If one sins, not a blunderer but a recidivist, minor as his offence is, he must be killed; if one commits a felony and repents, and it is accidental, just due to negligence, you should give him a proper penalty, but you shouldn't kill him."

The Lord said, "Ah, feoffee, to keep order is to practise the greatest conformance, and in this way the people will work diligently without committing crime. They will rid their wrongdoings like treating their diseases, and you should safeguard their well-being like protecting your own children. No one can punish or kill but you, no one can cut off someone's nose or ears but you."

The Lord said, "Ah, feoffee, only when the masses are on the right track can they all enjoy well-being. We should always keep in mind the virtuous governance of the previous kings and regard it as our ultimate goal to build a safe state with happy folks. This is especially true when the Yin people won't long for the better unless they are instructed, and unless they are instructed, there will be no good governance there."

The Lord said, "Ah, feoffee, be cautious! Don't cause resentment and don't let indiscreet illegitimate plans block your sincerity. Practise virtuous governance so that you will stay untroubled and your virtues will be remembered. Only when you study the right way to govern can the people feel assured, so they won't blame or overthrow you."

第四章　儒家
Chapter Ⅳ　Confucianism

第一节　《论语》
Section 1　*The Annalects*

1. 学而 Isn't It

子曰："学而时习之，不亦说乎？有朋自远方来，不亦乐乎？人不知而不愠，不亦君子乎？"

Confucius[①] said: "Isn't it a pleasure to acquire knowledge and practice it oftentimes? Isn't it a delight to have friends coming from afar? Isn't he a gentleman who doesn't sulk because others don't know him?"

有子曰："其为人也孝弟，而好犯上者，鲜矣；不好犯上，而好作乱者，未之有也。君子务本，本立而道生。孝弟也者，其为仁之本与！"

Yucius[②] said: "There are few who are pious to parents and brothers but apt to offend their superiors; there are none who would not offend their superiors but make trouble. A gentleman adheres to the foundation. When a foundation one lays, the Word pays. Piety is the foundation of benevolence."

---

① Confucius (551 B.C. – 479 B.C.): Born in Cou, the State of Lu in present-day Shandong, China, a greatest thinker and educator of all time. He toured and lobbied various states for 14 years with some of his disciples and compiled or revised six classics: *Poems*, *Book*, *Rites*, *Music*, *Changes*, and *Spring and Autumn* in his later years. He had 3000 disciples, of whom 72 were esteemed as sages. *Analects* is a collection of his and his disciples' remarks or dialogues, recorded and compiled by his disciples and/or his disciples' disciples. His doctrines have long developed into Confucianism, an important school of thought and an official religion in Chinese history.

② Yucius (518 B.C. – ?): Confucius's disciple, named Jo Yu, one of the two disciples who, like their teacher Confucius, were addressed as *cius*, which means master or teacher.

子曰："巧言令色，鲜矣仁!"

Confucius said: "Scarcely good are those who are plausible and flattering."

曾子曰："吾日三省吾身：为人谋而不忠乎？与朋友交而不信乎？传不习乎？"

Tsengcius[①] said: "I have three introspections a day: Am I not loyal to others? Am I not faithful with friends? Am I slack in my school work?"

子曰："道千乘之国，敬事而信，节用而爱人，使民以时。"

Confucius said: "In reining a state with one thousand chariots[②], one should be devoted to his work with great faith, economize on resources and love people, and work them at a proper time."

子曰："弟子入则孝，出则弟，谨而信，泛爱众而亲仁。行有余力，则以学文。"

Confucius said: "As a disciple, one should be pious to his parents at home and respectful to elders when out, abide by credit and love all souls, hence close to benevolence. If he has more energy to spare, he can go for literacy."

子夏曰："贤贤易色；事父母，能竭其力；事君，能致其身；与朋友交，言而有信。虽曰未学，吾必谓之学矣。"

Tsuhsia[③] said: "Revere sages as much as you love beauties, serve your parents at your best, serve the lord at your utmost. In dealing with your friends,

---

① Tsengcius (505 B.C. – 435 B.C.): Confucius's disciple, named San Tseng, one of the two disciples who, like their teacher Confucius, were addressed as *cius*, which means master or teacher.

② one thousand chariots: referring to a medium sized state or its military force. A chariot consists of 4 horses, 3 armored soldiers aboard, 72 infantrymen and 25 logisticians, 100 soldiers in total.

③ Tsuhsia (507 B.C. – ?): an alias for Shang Bu, from the State of Chin, one of Confucius's most famous disciples.

be faithful to your word. Even though you have not learned, I see it as good learning."

子曰："君子不重则不威，学则不固。主忠信。无友不如己者。过则勿惮改。"

Confucius said: "A gentleman, if not grave, is not powerful, nor well learned. Be loyal and faithful. Don't befriend those who are inferior to you. If you are wrong, don't fear to straighten up."

曾子曰："慎终追远，民德归厚矣。"

Tsengcius said: "Value our parents' funerals and remember our sires, so much so that the folks resume their simplicity."

子禽问于子贡曰："夫子至于是邦也，必闻其政，求之与？抑与之与？"子贡曰："夫子温、良、恭、俭、让以得之。夫子之求之也，其诸异乎人之求之与？"

Tsuch'in[①] asked Tsukung[②]: "When arriving in a state, our teacher must inquire about its governance. Does he ask for, or is he given, the honor?" Tsukung answered: "He gains it because of his clemency, conscience, respect, frugality and modesty. His way of gaining it is probably different from others, isn't it?"

子曰："父在，观其志；父没观其行；三年无改于父道，可谓孝矣。"

Confucius said: "Look at what a person wills if his father is living; look at what he does when his father is departed. He may be regarded as filial if he doesn't change his father's way for three years."

---

① Tsuch'in (508 B.C. – 430 B.C.): alias for Kang Ch'en, one of Confucius's disciples.

② Tsukung (520 B.C. – 456 B.C.): alias for Ts'u Duanmu, one of Confucius' s disciples.

有子曰："礼之用，和为贵。先王之道，斯为美；小大由之。有所不行，知和而和，不以礼节之，亦不可行也。"

Yucius said: "The use of rites lies in the focus on harmony. Our kings in olden days regarded it as graceful and observed it in matters small or great. In the case of inability to manage, it doesn't work to emphasize harmony for harmony's sake without the medium of rites."

有子曰："信近于义，言可复也。恭近于礼，远耻辱也。因不失其亲，亦可宗也。"

Yucius said: "If one's credibility adjoins righteousness, what he says can be trusted; if one's respect adjoins rites, he is away from shame or disgrace. Because he adheres to such virtues, one may follow him."

子曰："君子食无求饱，居无求安，敏于事而慎于言，就有道而正焉，可谓好学也已。"

Confucius said: "If a gentleman, not caring for food or housing, is diligent with what he does, careful with what he says and rectifies himself with a worthy, he can be regarded as a good learner."

子贡曰："贫而无谄，富而无骄，何如?"子曰："可也。未若贫而乐，富而好礼者也。"

子贡曰："《诗》云：'如切如磋，如琢如磨。'其斯之谓与?"子曰："赐也，始可与言《诗》已矣，告诸往而知来者。"

Tsukung asked: "What if one is poor but not flattering, rich but not proud?" Confucius replied: "That's good, but not as good as those who are poor but happy, rich but respectful." Tsukung replied: "As is said in *Poems*①, 'Like ivory

---

① *Poems*: also known as *She King* or *Book of Songs*, the earliest collection of poems in Chinese History.

polished, Like precious stone finished.' Is it what you mean?" Confucius answered: "You got it. Now I can teach you *Poems*, as I tell you the result, you know the wherefore."

子曰："不患人之不己知，患不知人也。"

Confucius said: "Don't worry others don't know you but worry you don't know others."

2. 为政 Governing

子曰："为政以德，譬如北辰居其所而众星共之。"

Confucius said: "Governing with virtue, like the Dipper, in its proper place and supported by all stars."

子曰："诗三百，一言以蔽之，曰：'思无邪。'"

Confucius said: "The three hundred[①] in *Poems* can be summarized in one phrase: 'free of evil thought.'"

子曰："道之以政，齐之以刑，民免而无耻。道之以德，齐之以礼，有耻且格。"

Confucius said: "If the masses are ruled with decrees and reined with penalties, they won't commit crime, but they won't feel shame either; if guided with virtues, and trained with rituals, they'll have a sense of shame, prone to submission."

子曰："吾十有五而志于学，三十而立，四十而不惑，五十而知天命，六十而耳顺，七十而从心所欲，不逾矩。"

Confucius said: "Such am I, determined to learn at fifteen, established at

① three hundred: an approximation of the 306 poems in *Poems*.

thirty, free from illusions at forty, knowing God's will at fifty, having a ready ear at sixty, and enjoying a free will without transgressing the boundaries at seventy."

孟懿子问孝。子曰："无违。"

樊迟御，子告之曰："孟孙问孝于我，我对曰，无违。"樊迟曰："何谓也?"子曰："生，事之以礼，死，葬之以礼，祭之以礼。"

Once Mengicius[①] inquired of Confucius about piety, who replied: "No transgression." Later Confucius told Fanch'i[②] who was driving for him: "Mengicius inquired of me about piety and I gave him the answer of no transgression." Fanch'i asked: "What is it?" Confucius answered: "Serve the living with rituals, bury the dead with rituals, and offer sacrifices with rituals."

孟武伯问孝。子曰："父母唯其疾之忧。"

To Mengwupo[③], who inquired about piety, Confucius replied: "Think how worried your parents are when you are ill."

子游问孝。子曰："今之孝者，是谓能养。至于犬马，皆能有养。不敬，何以别乎？"

To Tsuyu[④], who inquired about piety, Confucius replied: "Piety nowadays is regarded as taking care of our parents. But our dogs and horses we also take care of. Without veneration, what's the difference?"

子夏问孝。子曰："色难。有事，弟子服其劳；有酒食，先生馔，曾是以

① Mengicius (518 B.C. – 481 B.C.): the 9th suzerain of the Meng's of the State of Lu, Mencius' forefather, six generations before Mencius.

② Fanch'i (515 B.C. – ?): alias for Hsu Fan, one of Confucius's disciples.

③ Mengwupo: an archon in the State of Lu in the reign of Lord Ai, Mencius' forefather, six generations before Mencius.

④ Tsuyu (506 B.C. – ?): alias Yan Yan, from the State of Wu, one of Confucius's disciples, once a magistrate of Wu, a town of the State of Chin.

为孝乎？”

To Tsuhsia, who inquired about filiality, Confucius replied: “It’s hard to be sunny. As their child, one may take over their labor, and serve them liquor and food. Do you think it is filiality? ”

子曰：“吾与回言终日，不违，如愚。退而省其私，亦足以发，回也不愚。”

Confucius said: “I once talked with Hui Yan[①] for a whole day. He had no disagreement, as if foolish. When he retired, I observed what he did and found he could well apply what he had learned. Hui Yan is not foolish.”

子曰：“视其所以，观其所由，察其所安。人焉廋哉？人焉廋哉？”

Confucius said: “Look at what one has done, where he has gone, and how he has fun. Can he hide himself? Can he hide himself?

子曰：“温故而知新，可以为师矣。”

Confucius said: “If through review one knows more, he can be a teacher.”

子曰：“君子不器。”

Confucius said: “A gentleman is not to be a vessel.”

子贡问君子。子曰：“先行其言而后从之。”

Tsukung inquired about the being of a gentleman. Confucius replied: “Do before you say and say according to what you do. ”

子曰：“君子周而不比，小人比而不周。”

Confucius said: “Gentlemen team but do not scheme; flunkies scheme but

① Hui Yan (521 B.C. – 490 B.C.): Confucius’s best disciple, from the State of Lu, known for his diligence, modesty and faithfulness.

do not team."

子曰："学而不思则罔，思而不学则殆。"

Confucius said: "Learning without thinking, one strays; thinking without learning, one fails"

子曰："攻乎异端，斯害也已。"

Confucius said: "Going to extremes is harmful indeed."

子曰："由，诲汝知之乎！知之为知之，不知为不知，是知也。"

Confucius said: "Yu, do I have to tell you what knowing is? If you know, you know; if you don't know, you don't. It is knowing."

子张学干禄。子曰："多闻阙疑，慎言其余，则寡尤；多见阙殆，慎行其余，则寡悔。言寡尤，行寡悔，禄在其中矣。"

To Tsuchang[①] who inquired about how to be an official, Confucius replied: "Listen more, lay aside your doubt, and be careful with your words, then you commit few errors. Look more, lay aside what may be a trouble, and be careful with other things, then you have few regrets. Speak with few errors and do with few regrets, hence you find a good official in yourself,"

哀公问曰："何为则民服？"孔子对曰："举直错诸枉，则民服；举枉错诸直，则民不服。"

Lord Ai[②] asked: "What shall I do to submit the masses?" Confucius replied: "Keep what is right and discard what is wrong, then you'll see them submit; keep what is wrong and discard what is right, and you won't see them do."

---

① Tsuchang (503 B.C. – ?): alias for Shi Chuansun, from the State of Ch'en, one of Confucius's most famous disciples.

② Lord Ai (? – 468 B.C.), the 26th lord of the State of Lu, reigning from 494 B.C. to 468 B.C.

季康子问："使民敬、忠以劝，如之何？"子曰："临之以庄，则敬；孝慈，则忠；举善而教不能，则劝。"

Chik'angcius[①] asked: "How can I make people respectful and loyal and do their best?" Confucius answered: "Treat them with sincerity, and they will be respectful; give them the chance to be filial and loving, and they will be loyal; praise the worthy, raise the weak, and they will do their best."

或谓孔子曰："子奚不为政？"子曰："《书》云：'孝乎惟孝，友于兄弟，施于有政。'是亦为政。奚其为为政？"

Asked by somebody why he didn't become an official, Confucius replied: "According to *the Book*, what is piety is being filial to parents and kind to brothers, applicable to the state. It is serving the state. Why do I have to come out to serve the state?"

子曰："人而无信，不知其可也。大车无輗，小车无軏，其何以行之哉？"

Confucius said: "I don't know what a person can do with no credit. If a cart had no crossbar, and a dray had no reins, how could they go ahead?"

子张问："十世可知也？"子曰："殷因于夏礼，所损益，可知也；周因于殷礼，所损益，可知也。其或继周者，虽百世，可知也。"

Tsuchang asked: "Can we know what it may be ten generations later?" Confucius answered: "Shang's rites were adapted from Hsia's, the additions and subtractions you may see; Chough's rites were adapted from Shang's, the additions and subtractions you may see. What may come after Chough's you may see, even if it is something a hundred generations later."

---

① Chik'angcius (? – 468 B.C.), the prime minister of the State of Lu in the reign of Lord Ai, suzerain of one of the three most powerful families in the State of Lu, a man swaying power.

子曰："非其鬼而祭之，谄也。见义不为，无勇也。"

Confucius said: "If you pray to a ghost you needn't pray to, it is flattery; if you see what is right, but don't act, it is no bravery."

3. 述而 Retelling But

子曰："述而不作，信而好古，窃比于我老彭。"

Confucius said: "Retelling but not creating, believing and retrieving the past, I compare myself to Laocius① and Sire Peng②."

子曰："默而识之，学而不厌，诲人不倦，何有于我哉？"

Confucius said: "I muse in silence, learn without boredom, and teach without fatigue. Besides this, what do I have?"

子曰："德之不修，学之不讲，闻义不能徙，不善不能改，是吾忧也。"

Confucius said: "Virtue not reared, lessons not chewed, what's good not pursued, and what's bad not amended. This is what I worry about."

子之燕居，申申如也，夭夭如也。

Even if at leisure, Confucius is tidy, and he is cozy.

子曰："甚矣吾衰也！久矣吾不复梦见周公!"

Confucius said: "I'm so decrepit! It's long since I dreamed of Prince of Chough③ last."

---

① Laocius: a great philosopher and founder of Taoism. His only work, *The Word and the World*, is of the same importance with *the Bible*, *Physis* and *Vedas*.

② Sire Peng: a contemporary of Mound and Hibiscus, a gastronomist, a precursor of regimen and Taoism. He lived 800 years according to Kehung's *Biography of Immortals*.

③ Prince of Chough: A son of King Civil, brother of King Martial, a remarkable politician, military man, thinker, educator, and a forerunner of Confucianism.

子曰：“志于道，据于德，依于仁，游于艺。”

Confucius said: “Intent on the Word, based on the Virtue, clinging to clemency, and playing with the arts.”

子曰：“自行束脩以上，吾未尝无诲焉。”

Confucius said: “I never fail to teach anyone who’s willing to pay the required tuition.”

子曰：“不愤不启，不悱不发。举一隅不以三隅反，则不复也。”

Confucius said: “I will not illumine him if one’s not eager; I will not enlighten him if one’s not perplexed. If one cannot derive three from one, I won’t repeat. ”

子食于有丧者之侧，未尝饱也。

Eating by someone who’s lost a relative, Confucius never has enough.

子于是日哭，则不歌。

If having mourned, he never sings that day.

子谓颜渊曰：“用之则行，舍之则藏，唯我与尔有是夫！”

子路曰：“子行三军，则谁与？”

子曰：“暴虎冯河，死而无悔者，吾不与也。必也临事而惧，好谋而成者也。”

Confucius said to Hui Yan: “Employed, I will do; Unrequested, I will hide. Only you and I can do that!” Chungyu asked: “If you command an army, who would you work with?” Confucius answered: “I won’t work with the one who fights a tiger with fists, wades a river with no stick and is never repentant. My partner must be circumspect, calculating and fulfilling.”

子曰："富而可求也，虽执鞭之士，吾亦为之。如不可求，从吾所好。"

Confucius said: "If wealth can be sought after, I will do that even if I am made a valet de chambre. If it can't be sought after, I'll get on my own way."

子之所慎：齐、战、疾。

Teacher is careful with three things: fasting, war and illness.

子在齐闻《韶》，三月不知肉味，曰："不图为乐之至于斯也。"

In the State of Ch'i, Teacher forgot the taste of meat for months because he heard *Fair*, saying: "I've never expected the music is so bewitching."

冉有曰："夫子为卫君乎？"子贡曰："诺，吾将问之。"

入，曰："伯夷、叔齐何人也？"曰："古之贤人也。"曰："怨乎？"曰："求仁而得仁，又何怨？"出，曰："夫子不为也。"

Janyu asked: "Will Teacher assist Lord of Watch?" Tsukung replied: "All right, I'll ask him." He came in and asked: "Who were Po-e and Shuch'i?" Confucius answered: "Sages of yore." "Did they have grievances?" "They asked for virtue, and they got it. What grievances did they have?" Tsukung came out and answered Janyu: "Teacher will not do that."

子曰："饭疏食饮水，曲肱而枕之，乐亦在其中矣。不义而富且贵，于我如浮云。"

Confucius said: "Though eating coarse food, drinking water, my arm as my pillow, it is much fun. Wealth and ranks got through injustice are like floating clouds to me."

子曰："加我数年，五十以学《易》，可以无大过矣。"

Confucius said: "Give me a few more years, I will learn *Changes*① at 50, then I can be free of big errors."

子所雅言，《诗》、《书》、执礼，皆雅言也。

Confucius speaks standard language sometimes. He uses it in reading *Poems* and *the Book*②, and at ceremonies.

叶公问孔子于子路，子路不对。

子曰："女奚不曰：'其为人也，发愤忘食，乐以忘忧，不知老之将至云尔。'"

The Lord of She③ inquired Chungyu about Confucius. Chungyu didn't answer. Confucius said: "Why don't you tell him that a man like him forgets to eat when reading, so carefree and happy, not knowing he is getting old, such things like that?"

子曰："我非生而知之者，好古，敏以求之者也。"

Confucius said: "I am not a born savant. I love the past and I am diligent in learning."

子不语怪、力、乱、神。

Our teacher does not talk about spirits, ghosts or demons.

子曰："三人行，必有我师焉。择其善者而从之，其不善者而改之。"

Confucius said: In a company of three, my teacher there must be. The

---

① *Changes*: the most important source of philosophy, art and literature, a consummation of the thought or wisdom of ancient Chinese.

② *Book*: a prehistoric book recording prehistoric lords and their stories.

③ The Lord of She (550 B.C. – ?): Shen Ch'uliang, a militarist and statesman of the State of Ch'u, once a prime minister and minister of military affairs. His fief was She, therefore he was called the Lord of She.

worthy I choose and follow, and the unworthy I amend.

子曰："天生德于予，桓魋其如予何？"

Confucius said: "I've God-given power. What can Huantui[①] do to me?"

子曰："二三子以我为隐乎？吾无隐乎尔。吾无行而不与二三子者，是丘也。"

Confucius said: "Do you guys think I have something hidden from you? I've nothing hidden. I've nothing that cannot be shown to you. It is me."

子以四教：文、行、忠、信。

Confucius's teaching is based on four things: literature, conduct, faithfulness, and credit.

子曰："圣人，吾不得而见之矣；得见君子者，斯可矣。"

子曰："善人，吾不得见而之矣；得见有恒者，斯可矣。亡而为有，虚而为盈，约而为泰，难乎有恒矣。"

Confucius said: "A saint I have no chance to see; it's enough if I can see a gentleman." And he continued: "A worthy I have no chance to see; it's enough if I can see one who's persistent. Being in non-being, fullness in emptiness, peacefulness in poverty, this state is hard to keep."

子钓而不纲，戈不射宿。

Confucius angles for fish, not netting any; he shoots birds flying, not those in nests.

子曰："盖有不知而作之者，我无是也。多闻，择其善者而从之，多见而

① Huant'ui: a minister in the State of Sung in charge of military affairs, whose brother Ssumaniu was Confucius's disciple.

识之；知之次也。”

Confucius said: “There are such people who create though having no proper knowledge. I don’t do so. Listen a lot, choose the worthy and learn it; look a lot, and bear it in mind. This is the way to learn.”

互乡难与言，童子见，门人惑。子曰：“与其进也，不与其退也，唯何甚？人洁己以进，与其洁也，不保其往也。”

Huhsiang[①] was infamous. A boy from there came to pay Confucius a visit. The disciples were puzzled. Confucius said: “I commend his progress in stead of his retrogress. Why so hard on him! He’d clean himself to go ahead. I commend his cleanness, not covering up his past.”

子曰：“仁远乎哉？我欲仁，斯仁至矣。”

Confucius said: “Is benevolence far away? If I want to be benevolent, benevolence is here.”

陈司败问：“昭公知礼乎？”孔子曰：“知礼。”

孔子退，揖巫马期而进之，曰：“吾闻君子不党，君子亦党乎？君取于吴，为同姓，谓之吴孟子。君而知礼，孰不知礼？”

巫马期以告。子曰：“丘也幸，苟有过，人必知之。”

A justice from the State of Ch’en asked: “Does Lord Shao[②] observe rites?” Confucius answered “Yes.” When Confucius left, the justice bowed to Wumach’i[③], saying: “I hear a gentleman is not biased. But is a gentleman also biased? Lord Shao married a woman from the State of Wu. She, called Wumengcius, has the same family name with Lord Shao. If Lord Shao observes rites, who doesn’t?” Wumach’i reported this to Confucius, who exclaimed: “I am

① Huhsiang: a town unattested today.
② Lord Shao: the Lord of the State of Lu reigning from 541 B.C. to 510 B.C.
③ Wumach’i (521 B.C. – ?): one of Confucius’ disciples, a scholar.

lucky. If I make a mistake, it is known."

子与人歌而善，必使反之，而后和之。

Confucius asked one to sing together. If he sang well, Confucius must ask him to repeat and then join him.

子曰："文，莫吾犹人也。躬行君子，则吾未之有得。"

Confucius said: "In learning, probably I'm as good as others. But as a gentleman in practice, I am far from good."

子曰："若圣与仁，则吾岂敢？抑为之不厌，诲人不倦，则可谓云尔已矣。"公西华曰："正唯弟子不能学也。"

Confucius said: "Saintly or noble, how dare I claim to be? If one says I do without boredom and teach without fatigue, he may say that." Kunghsihua① exclaimed: "It is just what we disciples fall short of. "

子疾病，子路请祷。子曰："有诸？"子路对曰："有之。《诔》曰：'祷尔于上下神祇。'"子曰："丘之祷久矣。"

When Confucius was seriously ill, Chungyu would pray for him. Confucius asked: "Is there such a thing?" Chungyu answered: "Yes. *The Prayers* says: 'Pray to gods above and below.'" Confucius said: "I have been praying for long."

子曰："奢则不孙，俭则固。与其不孙也，宁固。"

Confucius said: "Extravagance leads to transgression, and economy to parsimony. But we prefer parsimony than transgression."

子曰："君子坦荡荡，小人长戚戚。"

Confucius said: "A gentleman strides up and down; a flunky cringes to

---

① Kunghsihua (509 B.C. or 519 B.C. – ?): one of Confucius's disciples, a scholar.

frown."

子温而厉，威而不猛，恭而安。

Confucius was mild and solemn, powerful but not awesome, respectful and composed.

第二节 《孟子》
Section 2 *Mencius*

1. 告子 Sir Teller

孟子曰："鱼，我所欲也；熊掌亦我所欲也；二者不可得兼，舍鱼而取熊掌者也。生，亦我所欲也；义，亦我所欲也；二者不可得兼，舍生而取义者也。生亦我所欲，所欲有甚于生者，故不为苟得也；死亦我所恶，所恶有甚于死者，故患有所不辟也。如使人之所欲莫甚于生，则凡可以得生者，何不用也？使人之所恶莫甚于死者，则凡可以辟患者，何不为也？由是则生而有不用也，由是则可以辟患而有不为也。是故所欲有甚于生者，所恶有甚于死者。非独贤者有是心也，人皆有之，贤者能勿丧耳。"

Mencius said: "Fish is what I want, so is bear's paw. If I cannot have both, I will pick bear's paw instead of fish. Life is what I want, so is righteousness. If I cannot have both, I will pick righteousness instead of life. Life is what I want, but there is something dearer than life, so I will not just remain alive. Death is what I detest, but there is something worse than death, so I am not in fear of a calamity. If nothing is more important than life, what cannot be done to keep their lives? If nothing is worse than death, what cannot be done to avoid a calamity? There are methods to keep alive, but none will apply them; there are ways to avoid a calamity, but none will take them. Therefore, one may desire something better than life and one may detest something more than death. Not only sages hold such a thought; everyone does. But sages will never lose it."

天将降大任于是人也，必先苦其心志，劳其筋骨，饿其体肤，空乏其身，行拂乱其所为，所以动心忍性，曾益其所不能。

Heaven, who will send him on a great mission, must first temper his will, work his bones, hunger his body, and deprive him of all so that nothing will derange his conduct, hence his perseverance will be strengthened and ability increased.

2. 公孙丑上 Ugly Lordson (Upper)

孟子曰："人皆有不忍人之心。先王有不忍人之心，斯有不忍人之政矣。以不忍人之心，行不忍人之政，治天下可运之掌上。所以谓人皆有不忍人之心者，今人乍见孺子将入于井，皆有怵惕恻隐之心——非所以内交于孺子之父母也，非所以要誉于乡党朋友也，非恶其声而然也。由是观之，无恻隐之心，非人也；无羞恶之心，非人也；无辞让之心，非人也；无是非之心，非人也。恻隐之心，仁之端也；羞恶之心，义之端也；辞让之心，礼之端也；是非之心，智之端也。人之有是四端也，犹其有四体也。有是四端而自谓不能者，自贼者也；谓其君不能者，贼其君者也。凡有四端于我者，知皆扩而充之矣，若火之始然，泉之始达。苟能充之，足以保四海；苟不充之，不足以事父母。"

Mencius said: "Everyone has compassion for others. Ancient kings had compassion for others, so they governed with policies of compassion. It is handy to govern with compassion for others and with policies of compassion. How to illustrate that everyone has compassion? When someone suddenly sees a child falling into a well, he must be stricken with scare and pity. This is not for the purpose of making friends with the child's parents or gaining a good reputation among his friends and countrymen or because of hating the cries of the child. Hence, with no compassion, one is no human; with no shame, one is no human; with no humility, one is no human; and with no sense of right and wrong, one is no human. Compassion is the beginning of benevolence; shame is the beginning of righteousness; humility is the beginning of propriety; the sense of right and wrong is the beginning of wisdom. People have these four beginnings, just like they have limbs. He who has these four beginnings but thinks that he cannot make them grow has done harm to himself; he who thinks that his lord cannot make them grow has harmed his lord. Those who realize that they have these four beginnings know how to expand them as if a fire had just begun to burn, as if a spring had just begun to spurt. If we can expand the four beginnings, it will be enough to stabilize the world. If we cannot expand them, we can't even serve our parents.

孟子曰："以力假仁者霸，霸必有大国；以德行仁者王，王不待大——汤以七十里，文王以百里。以力服人者，非心服也，力不赡也；以德服人者，中心悦而诚服也，如七十子之服孔子也。《诗》云：'自西自东，自南自北，无思不服。'此之谓也。"

Mencius said:"Only big states can seek hegemony through power and fake virtue. However, a state can conquer the world with good virtue and morality regardless of its size of territory." Hotspring started with a territory of 35 square kilometers, and King Civil 50. People don't really obey those who conquer others by force, only that they aren't powerful enough to rebel. However, you can have wholehearted obedience and respect from others with good virtue and morality, just like Confucius's 70 disciples who served their master. By doing so you can achieve what it is said in *the Book of Songs*: All come from east and west,/From north and from south and/Everywhere on the land."

3. 公孙丑下 Ugly Lordson (Lower)

孟子去齐，充虞路问曰："夫子若有不豫色然。前日虞闻诸夫子曰：'君子不怨天，不尤人。'"

曰："彼一时，此一时也。五百年必有王者兴，其间必有名世者。由周而来，七百有余岁矣。以其数，则过矣；以其时考之，则可矣。夫天未欲平治天下也，如欲平治天下，当今之世，舍我其谁也？吾何为不豫哉？”

Mencius left Ch’i and Yu Ch’ung asked him on the way, “Teacher, you seem unhappy. But I’ve heard you say the other day: “A gentleman doesn’t complain about Heaven or blame anyone.”

Mencius said, “Now it’s quite different from then. A sage king rises every 500 years, and there must be high-profile aides with him. It’s more than 700 years since King Martial of Chough. Now it is more than 500 years, and it is time for his coming. Maybe Heaven does not want a peaceful world. If he does, in today’s world, who else can but me? Why am I not happy?”

4. 梁惠王上 King Boon of Liang (Upper)

老吾老，以及人之老；幼吾幼，以及人之幼。天下可运于掌。《诗》云：“刑于寡妻，至于兄弟，以御于家邦。”言举斯心加诸彼而已。故推恩足以保四海，不推恩无以保妻子。古之人所以大过人者，无他焉，善推其所为而已矣。

Others’ parents are served as mine are served; others’ children are loved as mine are loved. This fulfilled, the whole world you may command. As *the Book of Songs* says: “By law his wife abode; his brothers kept the code; all folks followed the mode.” Therefore, if one extends his kindness to others, he will be able to appease the whole world, or he will not steadily support his wife and children. Why wise kings in ancient times exceeded far more than ordinary people is that they always extended their kindness.

5. 梁惠王下 King Boon of Liang (Lower)

孟子谓齐宣王曰：“王之臣有托其妻子于其友而之楚游者，比其反也，则冻馁其妻子，则如之何？”王曰：“弃之。”曰：“士师不能治士，则如之何？”王曰：“已之。”曰：“四境之内不治，则如之何？”王顾左右而言他。

Mencius talked to King Declare of Ch'i: "Suppose, Your Majesty has such an official. He will pay a visit to Ch'u and asks his friend to take care of his wife and children. When he comes back, he finds his family suffering from cold and hunger. What should be done to his friend?" King Declare replied: "Abandon him." Mencius asked: "What if a judicial official cannot manage his juniors well?" "Depose him." Mencius went on asking: "What if a king cannot manage his state well?" The king looked around and diverted the topic.

孟子见齐宣王，曰："所谓故国者，非谓有乔木之谓也，有世臣之谓也。王无亲臣矣，昔者所进，今日不知其亡也。"王曰："吾何以识其不才而舍之？"曰："国君进贤，如不得已，将使卑逾尊，疏逾戚，可不慎与？左右皆曰贤，未可也；诸大夫皆曰贤，未可也；国人皆曰贤，然后察之；见贤焉，然后用之。左右皆曰不可，勿听；诸大夫皆曰不可，勿听；国人皆曰不可，然后察之；见不可焉，然后去之。左右皆曰可杀，勿听；诸大夫皆曰可杀，勿听；国人皆曰可杀，然后察之；见可杀焉，然后杀之。故曰，国人杀之也。如此，然后可以为民父母。"

Mencius paid a formal visit to King Declare of Ch'i, saying: "An old state may not necessarily have tall trees, but it should have meritorious officials. Your Majesty does not have close ministers. Where are those appointed?" King Declare asked: "How can I know people who have no talent and abandon them?" Mencius answered: "In selecting officials, it may be unavoidable that a lord has the inferior exceed the noble, and the distant exceed the close, so can he not be careful about this? Whether a person is wise or not is not determined by the people around him or the ministers. When people all over the country say he is wise and able, it is time to investigate; if people all over the country suspect him, it is time to investigate, and if it is true, dismiss him. Similarly, whether a person should be killed or not is not determined by the people around him or by the ministers. When people all over the country say so, it is time to investigate, and if it is true, kill him. Then one can be a parent of the folks."

6. 尽心上 Heart and Soul (Upper)

孟子曰："莫非命也，顺受其正；是故知命者不立乎岩墙之下。尽其道而死者，正命也；桎梏死者，非正命也。"

Mencius said: "There's nothing that is not fate; it's right to accept what is right. Therefore, he who knows fate does not stand by a dangerous wall; he who follows the Word and dies has the right fate; he who dies in fetters does not."

杨子取为我，拔一毛而利天下，不为也。墨子兼爱，摩顶放踵利天下，为之。

What Chu Yang was for was self. If by plucking one hair he might benefit the whole world, he would not do it. What Sir Ink (Motzu) was for was universal love, if by hurting his body he might benefit the whole world, he would do it.

7. 尽心下 Heart and Soul (Lower)

民为贵，社稷次之，君为轻。是故得乎丘民而为天子，得乎天子为诸侯，得乎诸侯为大夫。诸侯危社稷，则变置。牺牲既成，粢盛既洁，祭祖以时，然而旱干水溢，则变置社稷。

People are the most valued; shrines the second, and lords the lightest. Those who win people will be a king; those who win a king will be vassals; those who win vassals will be officials. Vassals will be replaced if doing harm to the shrine; shrines will be replaced if sacrifices are sumptuous, clean and given in time but floods and droughts still sway.

第三节 《孝经》
Section 3 *Filial Piety*

1. 开宗明义 Introduction

夫孝，德之本也，教之所由生也。

Filial piety is the root of virtue, wherein grow teachings.

夫孝，始于事亲，中于事君，终于立身。

Filial piety begins with serving parents, grows in serving the ruler, and matures with establishing personality.

2. 圣治 Ruling the World with Filial Piety

天地之性，人为贵。人之行，莫大于孝。

Humans are the noblest between Heaven and earth. No other human conduct is better than filial piety.

3. 三才 Three Vitals

曾子曰："甚哉，孝之大也！"子曰："夫孝，天之经也，地之义也，民之行也。天地之经，而民是则之。则天之明，因地之利，以顺天下。是以其教不肃而成，其政不严而治。先王见教之可以化民也，是故先之以博爱，而民莫遗其亲；陈之以德义，而民兴行。先之以敬让，而民不争；导之以礼乐，而民和睦；示之以好恶，而民知禁。"

Tsengcius exclaimed: "Great, filial piety!" Confucius said: "Filial piety is the law of Heaven, the power of Earth, is the practice of humans. Heaven and earth runs its own natural law, from which humans learn the law they should follow. Following the constant law of Heaven and the four seasons, a king can administrate his people; in spite of his indulgent cultivation, he succeeds; in spite of his lenient administration, he governs. An ancient king saw that cultivation could enlighten commons, so he took the initiative to practice universal love, and there was no more abandonment of parents; he elaborated on the significance of ethics and rites, and the people followed; he showed respect and modesty, and there were no conflicts among people; he introduced rites and music, and people lived in harmony; he sorted the good out of the evil, and people became aware of what was prohibited by the law."

4. 广扬名 Ever-lasting Fame

子曰："君子之事亲孝，故忠可移于君；事兄悌，故顺可移于长；居家理，故治可移于官。是以形成于内，而名立于后世矣。"

Confucius said: "A gentleman serves his parents with filial piety, so he can change his filial piety into loyalty for the king; he treats his elder brothers with respect, so he can turn such respect into reverence for his seniors; he manages his household well, so he can turn such management into administration of the state. Therefore, those who do well at home will leave a good name to posterity."

5. 谏诤 Remonstrance

曾子曰："若夫慈爱、恭敬、安亲、扬名，则闻命矣。敢问子从父之令，可谓孝乎？"子曰："是何言与，是何言与！昔者天子有争臣七人，虽无道，不失其天下；诸侯有争臣五人，虽无道，不失其国；大夫有争臣三人，虽无道，不失其家；士有争友，则身不离于令名；父有争子，则身不陷于不义。故当不义，则子不可以不争于父；臣不可以不争于君；故当不义则争之。从父之令，又焉得为孝乎！"

Tsencius asked: "I have heard your teachings of loving, respecting, and sustaining parents, so as to be distinguished and remembered. May I venture to ask you again whether obeying a father's order is filial piety?" Confucius replied: "What are you talking about? What are you talking about? In the past, Sons of

Heaven had seven remonstrants, so they did not lose their kingdom even though they might have been fatuous; vassal lords had five remonstrants, so they did not lose their states even though they might have been fatuous; ministers or senior officials had three remonstrants, so they did not lose their fiefs, even though they might have been fatuous; literati had remonstrant friends, so they did not lose their reputation; fathers had remonstrant sons, so they were not trapped in immorality. When confronted with something immoral, it would not do for a son to keep silent in front of his father, and it would not do for subordinates to keep silent in front of kings. Therefore, in face of immorality, a son should admonish his father. If the son obeys his father, how can he be filial at all?"

6. 五刑 Five Punishments

五刑之属三千，而罪莫大于不孝。

Of three thousand offences in Five Punishments, none is more serious than filial impiety.

第五章 道家
Chapter V Wordism (Taoism)

第一节《道德经》
Section 1 *The Word and the World*

1. 第一篇 Chapter I

道可道，非常道；名可名，非常名。无名，天地之始；有名，万物之母。故常无欲，以观其妙；常有欲，以观其窍。此两者同出而异名，同谓之玄，玄之又玄，众妙之门。

The Word that can be worded is not the Word *per se*; the Name that can be named is not the Name proper. Nil is the name of the beginning of Heaven and Earth, and being, the name of the mother of all things. Therefore, without senses, one has access to subtlety, and with senses, one has access to demarcation. The two are of the same origin, the same but with different names. The profoundest of the profound is the entrance to all subtleties.

2. 第二篇 Chapter II

天下皆知美之为美，斯恶已；皆知善之为善，斯不善已。故有无相生，难易相成，长短相形，高下相倾，音声相和，先后相随。是以圣人处无为之事，行不言之教；万物作焉而不离，生而不有，为而不恃，功成而弗居；夫唯弗居，是以不去。

All the world know beauty is beauty, because of ugliness; all know goodness is goodness, because of non-goodness; what is nil and what is being generate each other; what is difficult and what is easy beget each other; what is long and what is short contrast each other; what is high and what is low complement each other; what is sound and what is voice attune each other; what is front and what is rear follow each other. This is what is eternal. Therefore, the sages leave things as they are. They teach without inculcation, let things arise instead of raising them; they work without deliberation, achieve without crediting themselves; just because they do not credit themselves, they have nothing to lose.

3. 第五篇 Chapter Ⅴ

天地不仁，以万物为刍狗；圣人不仁，以百姓为刍狗。天地之间，其犹橐籥乎？虚而不屈，动而愈出。多言数穷，不如守中。

Nature is unbiased, seeing everything as a straw dog; the sage is unbiased, seeing everyone as a straw dog. Isn't Nature like a bellows? Void, it's used without end; moved, the more it will send. Saying more than is done, no better than a mute one.

4. 第八篇 Chapter Ⅷ

上善若水。水，善利万物而不争，处众人之所恶，故几于道。

居善地，心善渊，与善仁，言善信，政善治，事善能，动善时。夫唯不争，故无尤。

The top goodness is like water, benefiting all, contending with none, and is content with all others disdain. Therefore, it is close to the Word.

It makes a good place, harbors a good will, gives a good wish, speaks good words, does good deeds, yields good results, and grasps good chance. Just because it does not contend, it never goes amiss.

5. 第九篇 Chapter Ⅸ

持而盈之，不如其已；揣而锐之，不可长保。金玉满堂，莫之能守。富贵而骄，自贻其咎。功成名遂，身退，天之道。

It is better to stop than to have it filled to slop; one cannot have it for long if it is too sharp. A houseful of treasures one cannot manage to keep; an overflow of riches and honors will cause a fall. It accords with nature if one retreats upon great success.

6. 第十二篇 Chapter XII

五色令人目盲，五音令人耳聋，五味令人口爽，驰骋田猎令人心发狂，难得之货令人行妨。是以圣人为腹不为目，故去彼取此。

Five colors dazzle the eyes, five sounds deafen the ears, five tastes baffle the palate, galloping to hunt drives one crazy, and rare goods reduce one to misconduct. Therefore, the saint cares for bellies rather than senses, keeping the former and checking the latter.

7. 第二十三篇 Chapter XXIII

希言自然。故飘风不终朝，骤雨不终日。孰为此者？天地。天地尚不能久，而况于人乎？故从事于道者：道者同于道， 德者同于德， 失者同于失。同于道者，道亦乐得之；同于德者，德亦乐得之；同于失者，失亦乐得之。信不足焉，有不信焉。

Reticence befits nature. Therefore, a high wind will not blow a whole morning; a big storm will not last a whole day. Who made them as they are? Heaven and Earth. Heaven and Earth cannot last long, let alone man? Therefore, he who follows the Word is with the Word; he who follows the virtue is with the virtue; he who follows the vice is with the vice. If one is with the Word, the Word will have him; if he is with the virtue, the virtue will have him; if one is with the vice, the vice will have him. If one is not trustworthy, none will trust him.

8. 第二十五篇 Chapter XXV

有物混成，先天地生，寂兮寥兮，独立而不改，周行而不殆，可以为天下母。吾不知其名，字之曰道，强为名之曰大。大曰逝，逝曰远，远曰反。故道大，天大，地大，王亦大。域中有四大，而王居其一焉。人法地，地法天，天法道，道法自然。

Something of chaos had earlier birth than Heaven and Earth. O soundless and formless, it does stand, extend, and recycle without end, which we may regard as Mother of the world. Her name I don't know, the Word you might call it, or Greatness if you insist on naming it. Greatness suggests "without end"; "without end" suggests "far away"; and "far away" suggests "recursion". Therefore, the Word is great; the Heaven is great, the earth is great, and man is also great. Out of the great four in the cosmos, man is one. Man is modeled on Earth, Earth on Heaven, Heaven on the Word, and the Word on Nature.

9. 第二十八篇 Chapter XXVIII

知其雄，守其雌，为天下溪；为天下溪，常德不离，复归于婴儿。知其白，守其黑，为天下式；为天下式，常德不忒，复归于无极。知其荣，守其辱，为天下谷；为天下谷，常德乃足，复归于朴。朴散则为器，圣人用之，则为官长，故大制不割。

Knowing it is a male, you keep the frail, willing to be a brook in the world. Being such a brook, you have virtue as e'er, back to babyhood. Knowing it is white, you keep the black, ready to be a model of the world. Being such a model, you ne'er commit errors, back to verity. Knowing it is a fame, you keep the shame, eager to be a vale in the world. Being such a vale, you have virtue enough, back to simplicity. With simplicity, utensils are made. With such, the sage can be a centurion, that is to say, great polity is undivided.

10. 第三十三篇 Chapter XXXIII

知人者智，自知者明，胜人者有力，自胜者强，知足者富，强行者有志，不失其所者久，死而不亡者寿。

He who knows others is wise; he who knows himself is bright; he who conquers others is forceful; he who conquers himself is strong; he who feels satisfied is rich; he who perseveres has a will; he who does not lose his due thrives; he who dies but still keeps the Word survives.

11. 第四十二篇 Chapter XXXXII

道生一，一生二，二生三，三生万物。万物负阴而抱阳，冲气以为和。人之所恶，孤、寡、不谷，而王公以为称。故物或损之而益，或益之而损。 人之所教，我亦教之：强梁者不得其死，吾将以为教父。

The Word begets one, one begets two, two beget three, and three beget everything. Everything carries Shade on its back and Shine in its arms, the opposites tending to harmony. Loneliness, helplessness, and worthlessness are what people detest while lords use them as their names. Therefore, to complement something, you deplete it; to deplete something, you complement it. As I am taught, so I teach. The strongest dies an unnatural death, This is an utmost lesson to learn.

12. 第四十五篇 Chapter XXXXV

大成若缺，其用不弊。大盈若冲，其用不穷。大直若屈，大巧若拙，大辩若讷。躁胜寒，静胜热，清静为天下正。

The great perfection seems to be defective, however, its uses are boundless; the great fullness seems to be empty, however, its uses are infinite. The great straightness seems to be crooked, the great nimbleness seems to be clumsy, and the great eloquence seems to be retarded. Still overrides fuss; cold overrides heat. Calmness is the best of all things.

13. 第四十八篇 Chapter XXXXVIII

为学日益，为道日损，损之又损，以至于无为，无为而无不为矣。故取天下者，常以无事；及其有事，不足以取天下。

For wits one does much; for the Word one undoes such. Undoing more and more until no ado. With no ado, one can everything do. One wins the world with no fuss, and with much fuss, one loses the world.

14. 第六十六篇 Chapter LXVI

江海所以能为百谷王者，以其善下之，故能为百谷王。是以圣人欲上人，必以言下之；欲先人，必以身后之。是以圣人处上而人不重，处前而人不害，是以天下乐推而不厌。以其不争，故天下莫能与之争。

The ocean can be the king of all rivers because it is located in a low place. Therefore, the sage, to rule the people, must use humble words, and to lead them, must place himself behind. Therefore, although the sage is above, the people do not feel burdened; although he is before them, they do not feel harmed. Therefore, all opt for him and do not feel fed up. It is because he does not contend that no one can contend with him.

15. 第六十七篇 Chapter LXVII

天下皆谓我大，似不肖。夫唯大，故似不肖；若肖，久矣其细也夫。我有三宝，持而宝之：一曰慈，二曰俭，三曰不敢为天下先。夫慈故能勇，俭故能广，不敢为天下先故能成器长。今舍慈且勇，舍俭且广，舍其后且先，死矣。夫慈，以战则胜，以守则固。天将救之，以慈卫之。

Everyone in the world claims that his Word is great, nothing like it. It is because it is great that nothing is like it. If something were like it, the Word would be insignificant! I have three treasures that I keep with me: one called kindness, the other frugality and the third the fear to be the first in the world. With kindness, one is brave; with frugality, one is generous; with fear to be the first in the world, one can be the leader of everything. Now without kindness, one tries to be brave, without frugality, one tries to be generous, and without reserve, one tries to be the first. The way to death! When kindness is applied to war, one can win, and applied to defense, one can guard. If Heaven helps one, it will protect him with kindness.

16. 第七十一篇 Chapter LXXI

知不知，上；不知知，病。夫唯病病，是以不病。圣人不病，以其病病，是以不病。

It is great if one knows something as if he doesn't know it; it is baneful if one doesn't know something as if he knows it. It is no fault just because one takes his fault as a fault. The sage has no fault. Just because he takes his fault as a fault, he has no fault.

17. 第七十八篇 Chapter LXXVIII

天下柔弱莫过于水，而攻坚强者莫之能胜，其无以易之。故弱胜强，柔胜刚，天下莫不知，莫能行。是以圣人云：‘受国之垢，是谓社稷主。受国之不祥，是为天下王。’正言若反。

In the world there is nothing weaker than water, but nothing can match it in conquering the hard and strong; nothing can replace it. Everyone knows that the weak can defeat the strong, the soft can defeat the hard, but nobody does likewise. Therefore, the sage says, "If bearing the shame of the state, you'll be the lord; if taking the bane of the state, you'll be the king." A paradox it is.

18. 第八十篇 Chapter LXXX

小国寡民，使有什伯人之器而不用，使民重死而不远徙。虽有舟车，无所乘之；虽有甲兵，无所陈之。使民复结绳而用之。甘其食，美其服，安其居，乐其俗。邻国相望，鸡犬之声相闻，民至老死不相往来。

Render the state small and the population sparse, so much so that they have no use for the weapons they have; incite the people to the fear of death so that they won't travel afar; though having boats and carts, they have no need to use them; though having soldiers, they have no chance to deploy them. Let the people go back to the olden days to live a simple life, tying knots for records, fed well, dressed well, settled well, and happy with the way they are. Across the state, people can gaze at each other, hearing chickens crow and dogs bark, but they do not have dealings with each other all their life.

第二节 《庄子》
Section 2 *Sir Lush*

1. 逍遥游第一 Chapter I : Flying Free

北冥有鱼，其名为鲲。鲲之大，不知其几千里也。化而为鸟，其名为鹏。鹏之背，不知其几千里也。怒而飞，其翼若垂天之云。是鸟也，海运则将徙于南冥。南冥者，天池也。

There in North Sea is a fish called Minnow, whose body spans about a thousand miles. When transformed into a bird, it is called Roc, whose back spans about a thousand miles. With a burst of vigor, it flies up, whose wings are like clouds hemming the sky. This bird, skimming tides, flies to South Sea. And this South Sea is called the Pool of IIcaven.

《齐谐》者，志怪者也。《谐》之言曰："鹏之徙于南冥也，水击三千里，抟扶摇而上者九万里，去以六月息者也。"野马也，尘埃也，生物之以息相吹也。天之苍苍，其正色邪，其远而无所至极邪？其视下也，亦若是则已矣。且夫水之积也不厚，则其负大舟也无力；覆杯水于坳堂之上，则芥为之舟；置杯焉则胶，水浅而舟大也。风之积也不厚，则其负大翼也无力。故九万里则风斯在下矣，而后乃今培风；背负青天而莫之夭阏者，而后乃今将图南。“蜩与学鸠笑之曰：‘我决起而飞，枪榆枋，时则不至，而控于地而已矣，奚以之九万里而南为？’”适莽苍者，三餐而反，腹犹果然；适百里者，宿舂粮；适千里者，三月聚粮。之二虫，又何知！小知不及大知，小年不及大年。奚以知其然也？朝菌不知晦朔，蟪蛄不知春秋，此小年也。楚之南有冥灵者，以五百岁为春，五百岁为秋；上古有大椿者，以八千岁为春，八千岁为秋。而彭祖乃今以久特闻，众人匹之，不亦悲乎？

Myth, a book of marvels and fables, says: “Roc flies to South Sea, splashing water for one thousand miles, whooping and whirling upwards for thirty thousand miles. It travels before the wind of the sixth moon.” The brume in the wilds or dust in the air is what is breathed out by living things. Is the azure the true color of the sky, or is it azure because of its boundless expanse? It is the same down below as high above.Water, if not deep enough, cannot well support a big boat. A cup of water poured to a hollow aground in a hall can carry a blade of grass as a boat; if the cup is placed there, it’ll be stuck to the floor, because the water is too shallow and the boat is too big. Wind, if not high enough, cannot uphold big wings. Therefore, thirty thousand miles above, Roc has wind below it, and with the help of the wind, it flies across the blue sky to South Sea without hindrance. A cicada and a little turtledove laugh at Roc: “I fly up with might to an elm or ebony, and if I can’t reach it sometimes, I just alight aground, why travel three thousand miles to South Sea?” If one goes to a pasture, a preparation of three meals is enough, and when he comes back, he still feels full; if one goes as far as thirty miles, he need grind rice for a whole night; if one goes as far as three hundred miles, he need prepare food for three months. How can they know this, such small things as cicadas and turtledoves? Those who know little can’t compare with those who know much; those who live short can’t compare with those who live long. How can they know such? Fungus knows no night or morning; cicadas know no spring or autumn, because they live short. South of Ch’u, there is a tree called Immortal Turtle, which regards five hundred years as spring and five hundred years as autumn. In ancient times, there was a tree called Giant Toon, which regarded eight thousand years as spring and eight thousand years as autumn. And, Sire Peng is famous for his longevity. Isn't it pitiable if people today would compare with him?

汤之问棘也是已："穷发之北，有冥海者，天池也。有鱼焉，其广数千里，未有知其修者，其名为鲲。有鸟焉，其名为鹏，背若太山，翼若垂天之云，抟扶摇羊角而上者九万里，绝云气，负青天，然后图南，且适南冥也。斥鴳笑之曰：'彼且奚适也？我腾跃而上，不过数仞而下，翱翔蓬蒿之间，此亦飞之至也，而彼且奚适也？'"此小大之辩也。

It was the same matter that Hotspring consulted Thorn about. Thorn replied: "It is boundless out of the boundless stretch. North the barren wildness there's a broad sea, which is the Pool of Heaven. There's in it a fish whose back is about one thousand miles in width. As for its length, nobody knows. Its name is Minnow. And there's a bird called Roc, whose back is as big as Mt. Arch, and whose wings are like clouds hemming the sky. It whooshes up for three thousand miles, penetrating the mist, and carrying the blue sky on its back, it flies south, towards South Sea. The sparrow in the small bog sneers at it: 'Where is it flying? I hop and fly up, just a dozen feet. I have a good flight, hovering above bushes. Where is it flying?'" This is the difference between what's big and what's small.

故夫知效一官，行比一乡，德合一君而征一国者，其自视也，亦若此矣。而宋荣子犹然笑之。且举世而誉之而不加劝，举世而非之而不加沮，定乎内外之分，辩乎荣辱之境，斯已矣。彼其于世，未数数然也。虽然，犹有未树也。夫列子御风而行，泠然善也，旬有五日而后反；彼于致福者，未数数然也。此虽免乎行，犹有所待者也。若夫乘天地之正，而御六气之辩，以游无穷者，彼且恶乎待哉！故曰：至人无己，神人无功，圣人无名。

Therefore, he who is equal to a position, able to safeguard a town, and pleasant to the lord with his virtues, hence trusted by all in the state, just thinks himself like this. At such people Sir Glory of Sung laughs. He is not encouraged even if praised by the whole world; he is not disheartened even if slandered by the whole world. He knows the confines of all and himself and knows the bounds of honor and humiliation. That's it. He does not buckle down to anything in the world, and yet there's still something he has not attained. Sir Line surfs the air, happy and free, and he returns in fifteen days. He is not intent on a gain of bliss. Though he is airborne, he's still reliant on something. If compliant with the nature of everything under the sun, commanding the change of air, soaring across the boundless space, what else does he have to lay hold on? Therefore, an ace seeks no honor; a sage seeks no merits; a saint seeks no fame.

尧让天下于许由，曰："日月出矣，而爝火不息，其于光也，不亦难乎！时雨降矣，而犹浸灌，其于泽也，不亦劳乎！夫子立而天下治，而我犹尸之，吾自视缺然，请致天下。"

Mound said when demising his throne to Freedom: "The sun is up but the torch is still on. Isn't it hard for its light to compare with that of the sun? When it rains timely, isn't it a waste of effort to go on watering a field? If you are in the position, the state will be prosperous. If I'm still here, I won't feel I can manage, please take it."

许由曰："子治天下，天下既已治也，而我犹代子，吾将为名乎？名者，实之宾也。吾将为宾乎？鹪鹩巢于深林，不过一枝；偃鼠饮河，不过满腹。归休乎君，予无所用天下为。庖人虽不治庖，尸祝不越樽俎而代之矣！"

Freedom replied: "Under your rule, the state has been prosperous. If I take your place, do I take it for a good name? A name is secondary to the named. Shall I do what is secondary? A wren in a wood just needs one branch to build its nest on; a mole that goes to a river to drink but fills its stomach with water. Please go back. Reining the world means nothing to me. Even if a cook does not work, a priest will not cook in his stead!"

肩吾问于连叔曰："吾闻言于接舆，大而无当，往而不返。吾惊怖其言，犹河汉而无极也；大有迳庭，不近人情焉。"连叔曰："其言谓何哉？"曰："'藐姑射之山有神人居焉，肌肤若冰雪，绰约若处子；不食五谷，吸风饮露；乘云气，御飞龙，而游乎四海之外；其神凝，使物不疵疠而年谷熟。'吾以是狂而不信也。"

Shoulder Defense said to Chain Third: "I heard what Cart Joiner talked about, so improper and irrelevant. I was startled with what he said, which was like the limitless Milky Way, so absurd and senseless." And Chain Third replied: "What did he say?" "'There in the Girl Archer Mountains lives an immortal, whose skin is as pure as snow, and who is as supple as a virgin. He eats no grains but imbibes clean air and dew, and he, astride a dragon, soars beyond the four seas. He gazes carefully so that there will be a bumper harvest, free of harms.' I think it so crazy and unbelievable."

连叔曰："然。瞽者无以与乎文章之观，聋者无以与乎钟鼓之声。岂唯形骸有聋盲哉！夫知亦有之。是其言也，犹时女也。之人也，之德也，将旁礴万物以为一，世蕲乎乱，孰弊弊焉以天下为事！之人也，物莫之伤，大浸稽天而不溺，大旱金石流、土山焦而不热。是其尘垢秕糠，将犹陶铸尧舜者也，孰肯以物为事！宋人资章甫而适诸越，越人断发文身，无所用之。尧治天下之民，平海内之政，往见四子藐姑射之山、汾水之阳，窅然丧其天下焉。"

And Chain Third went on: "Yes, a blind man can't enjoy beautiful colors; a deaf-mute can't enjoy the sound of bells and drums. Is one just physically blind or deaf? He may be blind spiritually. What you said now is just insipid as before. That man, that worth, he is the one unified with everything in nature. Will he take the trouble to manage trivialities of the world? This man nothing can hurt. Even a deluge cannot drown him; even a drought that melts gold and stone and burns hills cannot choke him. He can even make great kings with dirt, dust or chaff. Will he trouble about worldly affairs?" A man from the State of Sung bought caps and went to Yüeh to sell them. The Yüeh people, however, had no use for them because they wore tattoos with their hair cut midway. Mound, having governed all people well and pacified all the states, went to see the four sages in the Girl Archer Mountains and on the north bank of River Fen. There he felt quite at loss, as if he had lost all in the world."

惠子谓庄子曰："魏王贻我大瓠之种，我树之，成，而实五石；以盛水浆，其坚不能自举也；剖之以为瓢，则瓠落无所容。非不呺然大也，吾为其无用而掊之。"庄子曰："夫子固拙于用大矣。宋人有善为不龟手之药者，世世以洴澼絖为事。客闻之，请买其方百金。聚族而谋曰：'我世世为洴澼絖，不过数金；今一朝而鬻技百金，请与之。'客得之，以说吴王。越有难，吴王使之将；冬，与越人水战，大败越人，裂地而封之。能不龟手一也，或以封，或不免于洴澼絖，则所用之异也。今子有五石之瓠，何不虑以为大樽而浮乎江湖，而忧其瓠落无所容？则夫子犹有蓬之心也夫！"

Sir Good told Sir Lush: "Lord Way gave me a gourd seed, and I sowed it. A gourd it bore was 30 meters across. If used for storage of water, it wouldn't be strong enough; if made into a dipper, it would be too big to be put anywhere. It was not the case that the gourd was not big but that I had no use for it, so I broke it." Sir Lush said: "You, my friend, are not good at big things. A man in Sung was good at concoction of medicine for chapped hands. From generation to generation, his family washed yarn for a living. A traveler, hearing of this, would buy the prescript for a hundred taels of gold. The prescript owner gathered his family for a discussion, saying: 'We've washed yarn for generations and earned but a few taels; today, if we sell the prescript, we can get a hundred at once, why not sell it?' The traveler bought it and lobbied the king of Wu. And right then the State of Yüeh was attacking the State of Wu, so the King of Wu made him a general. That winter, he defeated the Yüeh army in a battle on water, and was therefore granted with a fief because he had used the medicine as a preventive against chapped hands. The same medicine, one used it and got a fief, and the other used it just for yarn washing. Different applications! Now you have a gourd 30 meters across, why not make it into a boat to tour a river or a lake? Why worry it's too big? Aren't you so short sighted? "

惠子谓庄子曰："吾有大树，人谓之樗，其大本拥肿而不中绳墨，其小枝卷曲而不中规矩，立之涂，匠者不顾。今子之言，大而无用，众所同去也。"庄子曰："子独不见狸狌乎？卑身而伏，以候敖者；东西跳梁，不辟高下，中于机辟，死于罔罟。今夫斄牛，其大若垂天之云。此能为大矣，而不能执鼠。今子有大树，患其无用，何不树之于无何有之乡，广莫之野，彷徨乎无为其侧，逍遥乎寝卧其下；不夭斤斧，物无害者，无所可用，安所困苦哉！"

Then Sir Good told Sir Lush: "I have a giant tree called toon. Its trunk, with lots of warts, can't be gauged; its branches are too twisted to be measured. Standing wayside, it has no carpenter's regard. Now you have talked too big to be useful. All will discard it." Sir Lush said: "Haven't you, sir, seen wild cats and weasels lurching for small animals; they jump east or west, leap high or low and fall into traps, left to die there. And there are cattle that are as big as clouds hemming the sky. They are powerful, but too powerful to catch mice. Now you have a big tree and worry that you have no use for it. Why not plant it in some place that is barren and boundless? You may wander around it and lie at leisure under it. There is no ax aimed at it; nothing can harm it. Isn't it carefree though useless?"

2. 齐物论第二 Chapter Ⅱ: Identified as One

南郭子綦隐机而坐，仰天而嘘，荅焉似丧其耦。颜成子游立侍乎前，曰："何居乎？形固可使如槁木，而心固可使如死灰乎？今之隐机者，非昔之隐机者也。"子綦曰："偃，不亦善乎，而问之也！今者吾丧我，汝知之乎！女闻人籁而未闻地籁，女闻地籁而未闻天籁夫！"

Sir Black Southend sat by a table, breathing air to the sky, looking hollow as if having lost himself. Sir Tour Goodlook, standing in front for company, said: “What’s the matter? A body can be made like a rotten log, but can a mind be made like ash? You are different from what you were, sitting by the same table.” Sir Black replied: “What a good question to ask! I’ve forgotten myself today, you know? You may have heard the sound of man but not the sound of earth; you may have heard the sound of earth but not the sound of Heaven!”

子游曰：“敢问其方。”子綦曰：“夫大块噫气，其名为风。是唯无作，作则万窍怒呺。而独不闻之翏翏乎？山林之畏佳，大木百围之窍穴，似鼻，似口，似耳，似枅，似圈，似臼，似洼者，似污者；激者，謞者，叱者，吸者，叫者，譹者，宎者，咬者。前者唱于，而随者唱喁。泠风则小和，飘风则大和，厉风济则众窍为虚。而独不见之调调、之刁刁乎？”子游曰：“地籁则众窍是已，人籁则比竹是已。敢问天籁。”子綦曰：“夫吹万不同，而使其自已也，咸其自取，怒者其谁邪？”

Sir Tour requested: “Please tell me the import.” Sir Black continued: “What the earth exhales is called wind. Wind may be quiet, but when it blows, countless crevices on the earth begin to howl. Haven’t you heard the whirs? The peaks and crags of hills and the orifices of giant trees look like a nose, a mouth, or an ear, like a cavity, a fence, a mortar, a pool or a pond, some gurgling, some darting, some shouting, some murmuring, some crying, some cawing, some echoing, some chirping, that in the front conducting, and that before him performing. A gentle air has mild concord; a high wind has great concord. When a gale stops suddenly, all things are hushed. Haven’t you seen that everything sways when a wind blows?” And Sir Tour asked again: “The sound of earth is what is exhaled from myriads of crevices, and the sound of man is what is blown out from various flutes, may I ask you what the sound of Heaven is?” Sir Black replied: “The blowing may be vastly diverse, but it starts or stops all by itself. Who else can set it off?”

大知闲闲，小知间间；大言炎炎，小言詹詹。其寐也魂交，其觉也形开。与接为搆，日以心斗。缦者，窖者，密者。小恐惴惴，大恐缦缦。其发若机栝，其司是非之谓也；其留若诅盟，其守胜之谓也；其杀若秋冬，以言其日消也；其溺之所为之，不可使复之也；其厌也如缄，以言其老洫也；近死之心，莫使复阳也。喜怒哀乐，虑叹变慹，姚佚启态。乐出虚，蒸成菌。日夜相代乎前，而莫知其所萌。已乎，已乎！旦暮得此，其所由以生乎！

Those of gifts wander free; those with wits but bits see. The words from the Word glare; the words from the tongue flare. When they sleep, their spirit meets their soul; when they awake, their limbs spread apart; when dealing with the world, they intrigue and complicate. Some are tardy, some are mystic, and some are circumspect. The short is shocked; the big is shaken. When they speak, their words are like arrows, good or evil; what they keep is kept like vows, to be set off when it is advantageous; when they wither like autumn grass, they shrivel day by day; they indulge in what they do, unable to come out; they are shut as if bound with a rope, they are left to age fast; on the verge of death, they can't be rejuvenated. They are glad, angry, sad, and gleeful; they muse, they sigh, they fidget, and they fear; they are rash, flashy, crazy and artificial; they are like notes blown out, like fungi mushrooming. Produced and reproduced, they don't know how it happens. Forget it, forget it! If they know how it happens, they know the cause and effect of it!

非彼无我，非我无所取。是亦近矣，而不知其所为使。若有真宰，而特不得其眹。可行已信，而不见其形，有情而无形。

There's no subject without object; there's no object without subject. It is close to things as they are, but we don't know what makes them what they are. There seems to be a real lord, but we can't even find his trace. We can try to prove his existence but we can't see his figure, a soul without form.

百骸、九窍、六藏，赅而存焉，吾谁与为亲？汝皆说之乎？其有私焉？如是皆有为臣妾乎？其臣妾不足以相治乎？其递相为君臣乎？其有真君存焉？如求得其情与不得，无益损乎其真。

Hundreds of condyles, nine cavities, and six viscera all exist in me. Which is my favorite? Do you like all those of yours or are your partial to some of them? Are they all your concubines? Can they rule each other or can they each be a ruler in turn? Is there really a ruler among them? Whether you can find it or not, there will be no harm or good done to it.

一受其成形，不忘以待尽。与物相刃相靡，其行尽如驰，而莫之能止，不亦悲乎！终身役役而不见其成功，苶然疲役而不知其所归，可不哀邪！人谓之不死，奚益？其形化，其心与之然，可不谓大哀乎！人之生也，固若是芒乎？其我独芒，而人亦有不芒者乎？

Once formed, one cannot wait to die without doing something. For or against the world, he runs or gallops as if none can stop him. Isn't it a tragedy? He labors all his life without seeing a success; he toils and moils all day without knowing his end. Isn't it so sad? Someone may say such a person will not die, but what's the use of that? His body declines, so does his mind. Isn't it a great curse? Is human life such a puzzle? Am I puzzled alone while others are not?

夫随其成心而师之，谁独且无师乎？奚必知代而心自取者有之？愚者与有焉。未成乎心而有是非，是今日适越而昔至也。是以无有为有。无有为有，虽有神禹且不能知，吾独且奈何哉！

If one follows his bias and regards it as his teacher, who does not have a teacher? Why only those who learn and acquire something have a teacher? Even a fool may have one. If one is not able to make judgment but can tell right from wrong, it is just like leaving for the State of Yüeh today, one arrived there yesterday. It is just the case that non-being is regarded as being. If non-being is regarded as being, even a person as saintly as Worm cannot understand it. What on earth can I do?

夫言非吹也。言者有言，其所言者特未定也。果有言邪，其未尝有言邪？其以为异于鷇音，亦有辩乎，其无辩乎？

A talk is not a blow. A talker talks on, and what he talks about remains unproven. Is there anything talked about or is there nothing talked about? One may regard his speech different from chirps of fledglings. Is there any difference or no difference at all?

道恶乎隐而有真伪？言恶乎隐而有是非？道恶乎往而不存？言恶乎存而不可？道隐于小成，言隐于荣华。故有儒墨之是非，以是其所非而非其所是。欲是其所非而非其所是，则莫若以明。

How does the Word hide, hence truth and falsity? How does a talk hide, hence sense and nonsense? How does the Word appear and then disappear? How does a talk exist and then perish? The Word is covered with trivial merits; the talk is veiled with flashy words. Therefore, there arise disputes between Confucianism and Inkism. One affirms what the other negates and negates what the other affirms. If one takes the trouble to affirm what the other negates, he may as well look at things as they are.

物无非彼，物无非是。自彼则不见，自知则知之。故曰彼出于是，是亦因彼。彼是方生之说也。虽然，方生方死，方死方生；方可方不可，方不可方可；因是因非，因非因是。是以圣人不由而照之于天，亦因是也。是亦彼也，彼亦是也。彼亦一是非，此亦一是非。果且有彼是乎哉，果且无彼是乎哉？彼是莫得其偶，谓之道枢。枢始得其环中，以应无穷。是亦一无穷，非亦一无穷也。故曰莫若以明。

Each contains that side; each contains this side. If one can't see this side, he can't see that side, either; if he knows this side, he knows that side as well. Therefore, that is begotten from this, and this is traced to that. This and that live on each other. On the other hand, one is born the moment he dies; one dies the moment he is born. He agrees and then disagrees; he disagrees and then agrees. Abiding by what is right is abiding by what is wrong; abiding by what is wrong is abiding by what is right. Therefore, a sage does not take sides but relies on Heaven and sees things as they are. This is also that; that is also this. That is both right and wrong; this is both right and wrong. Do there really exist that and this? Don't there really exist that and this? What does not have a mate is called a central hub. A central hub is the point leading to infinitude. What is right is infinitude; what is wrong is infinitude. Therefore, it is best to look at things as they are.

以指喻指之非指，不若以非指喻指之非指也；以马喻马之非马，不若以非马喻马之非马也。天地一指也，万物一马也。

Using a thumb to prove a thumb is not a thumb is not as good as using a non-thumb to prove a thumb is not a thumb; using a horse to prove a horse is not a horse is not as good as using a non-horse to prove a horse is not a horse. The universe is a thumb; everything is a horse.

可乎可，不可乎不可。道行之而成，物谓之而然。恶乎然？然于然。恶乎不然？不然于不然。物固有所然，物固有所可。无物不然，无物不可。故为是举莛与楹，厉与西施，恢恑憰怪，道通为一。

You agree because you're willing to; you don't agree because you aren't willing to. A pass comes into being because people pass here; something is so called because people call it so. Is it right? It is right because it is right in itself. Is it not right? It is not right because it is not right in itself. Everything has something inherent to it; everything has something agreeable to it; nothing hasn't something inherent to it; nothing hasn't something agreeable to it. Therefore, a stem and a column, a hag and a belle, what is large or queer and what is crafty or monstrous, are all unified in the Word.

其分也，成也；其成也，毁也。凡物无成与毁，复通为一。唯达者知通为一，为是不用，而寓诸庸。庸也者，用也；用也者，通也；通也者，得也；适得而几矣。因是已。已而不知其然，谓之道。劳神明为一，而不知其同也，谓之“朝三”。何谓“朝三”？狙公赋芧，曰：“朝三而暮四。”众狙皆怒。曰：“然则朝四而暮三。”众狙皆悦。名实未亏，而喜怒为用，亦因是也。是以圣人和之以是非，而休乎天钧，是之谓两行。

Something's complete the moment it's divided; something's destroyed the moment it's complete. Nothing is complete or destroyed; all return to one. Only the perspicacious know the identification of one, therefore he's not bigoted as if owning all. Owning is using; using is moving; moving is getting. It's enough to get enough. Following the course and not knowing the cause is called the Word. Trying to know the One without knowing everything is the same one is called "three in the morning". What's it? A monkey keeper fed his monkeys with acorns, saying: "Three in the morning and four in the evening." The monkeys got angry. And the keeper said: "Then you have four in the morning and three in the evening." All the monkeys were pleased. Nothing was changed in name or in fact, but the monkeys felt affected due to their own understanding. Therefore, a sage identifies rights with wrongs and rests assured with the balance of Heaven, which is called Felicity of the Two.

古之人，其知有所至矣。恶乎至？有以为未始有物者，至矣，尽矣，不可以加矣。其次以为有物矣，而未始有封也。其次以为有封焉，而未始有是非也。是非之彰也，道之所以亏也。道之所以亏，爱之所之成。果且有成与亏乎哉，果且无成与亏乎哉？有成与亏，故昭氏之鼓琴也；无成与亏，故昭氏之不鼓琴也。昭文之鼓琴也，师旷之枝策也，惠子之据梧也，三子之知几乎，皆其盛者也，故载之末年。唯其好之也，以异于彼；其好之也，欲以明之。非所明而明之，故以坚白之昧终。而其子又以文之纶终，终身无成。若是而可谓成乎？虽我亦成也。若是而不可谓成乎？物与我无成也。是故滑疑之耀，圣人之所图也。为是不用而寓诸庸，此之谓以明。

The ancients consummated their wisdom. What's that? Some believed that in the beginning there was nothing. How pithy, how perfect! It can't be better! And some with less acumen believed that there was something but it was undivided. And the next believed that there was something, divided but not distinguished as right or wrong. The revelation of right and wrong causes the inadequacy of the Word. The inadequacy is due to our prejudices. Is there really such a thing as perfection or inadequacy? Is there really such a thing as imperfection or inadequacy? With such things as perfection and inadequacy, Mr. Bright could play the lute; without, he couldn't. Mr. Bright's performance, Master Broad's prosody and Sir Good's monologue by a Chinese parasol tree were all consummate because of their topmost talents, hence recorded in history books. Just because of their aptitude, they were distinguished from others, and because of their aptitude, they would display it. If one displays what he shouldn't, he'll end up with such folly as "Hard-or-white". Bright's son succeeded him but didn't succeed at all. Can this case be called a success? If so, I can also be seen as successful. Can this case not be called a success? The world and I have no success to speak of. Therefore, the display of mesmerizing plausibility is what sages disregard. Therefore, non-use is embodied in use, as is called Brightness.

今且有言于此，不知其与是类乎，其与是不类乎？类与不类，相与为类，则与彼无以异矣。虽然，请尝言之。有始也者，有未始有始也者，有未始有夫未始有始也者。有有也者，有无也者，有未始有无也者，有未始有夫未始有无也者。俄而有无矣，而未知有无之果孰有孰无也。今我则已有谓矣，而未知吾所谓之其果有谓乎，其果无谓乎？

So far, I have talked like this. I don't know whether it is the same kind with, or a different kind from, others' talks. The same kind or different kinds? As we all talk, we are the same kind, hence no difference from other talks. Nevertheless, please allow me to talk a little more. Suppose a beginning there, a beginning of what's not yet begun, and a beginning of what's not yet begun of what's not yet begun. A being of what's a being, a being of what's a non-being, a being of what's a non-being of what's not yet begun, and a being of what's a non-being of what's not yet begun of what's not yet begun. Suddenly there prop up being and non-being, but I don't know which of them is really being or non-being. Now I have talked, but I don't know whether I have talked at all or haven't talked at all.

天下莫大于秋豪之末，而太山为小；莫寿于殇子，而彭祖为夭。天地与我并生，而万物与我为一。既已为一矣，且得有言乎？既已谓之一矣，且得无言乎？一与言为二，二与一为三。自此以往，巧历不能得，而况其凡乎！故自无适有，以至于三，而况自有适有乎！无适焉，因是已。

Nothing under the sun is as large as a tiny bit; a high mountain is small; none is as long lived as a child who dies prematurely; none is as short lived as Sire Peng, the immortal. Heaven and earth live with me; all things are identified with me. Since we are one, is there anything as a talk? Since we are called one, is there anything as a non-talk? One and I make two; two and one make three. In a similar fashion, even the wisest calculator cannot have a final sum, let alone an ordinary person. From non-being to being, then three, let alone from being to being. It's unnecessary to go on, leave it as it is.

夫道未始有封，言未始有常，为是而有畛也。请言其畛：有左有右，有伦有义，有分有辩，有竞有争，此之谓八德。六合之外，圣人存而不论；六合之内，圣人论而不议。《春秋》经世先王之志，圣人议而不辩。故分也者，有不分也；辩也者，有不辩也。曰：何也？圣人怀之，众人辩之以相示也。故曰，辩也者，有不见也。

The Word has no sections, nor has speech criteria. Self-assertion results in boundaries. Please allow me to talk about boundaries. Left, right, sequence, altitude, argument, refutation, emulation, and contention are called eight categories. What is beyond the universe a saint beholds but does not talk about; what is within he studies but does not remark on. The annals of early kings a saint studies but does not argue about. Therefore, there's something divided and there's something undivided; there's something argued about and there's something not argued about. You may ask why. A saint keeps them in mind while the masses argue about them and display them. Therefore, it's said one argues because there's something he fails to see.

夫大道不称，大辩不言，大仁不仁，大廉不嗛，大勇不忮。道昭而不道，言辩而不及，仁常而不成，廉清而不信，勇忮而不成。五者圆而几向方矣。故知止其所不知，至矣。孰知不言之辩，不道之道？若有能知，此之谓天府。注焉而不满，酌焉而不竭，而不知其所由来，此之谓葆光。

The great Word is not named; a great speech is not uttered; great humanity is not shown; great integrity is not modest; great courage is not assuming. The Word, if evident, is not the Word; a speech, if uttered, is not inclusive; humanity, if revealed, is not enduring; integrity, if obvious, is not trustable; courage, if assuming, is not real courage. If one fully considers these five, he is in the right direction. Therefore, if one stops at what he doesn't know, he is the wisest. Who knows the unuttered speech and the unspoken Word? If one knows, he is back to what's called a Heavenly hoard. Fill it, and it's not filled; take it, and it's not exhausted. However, we don't know its source. This can be called reserved light.

故昔者尧问于舜曰："我欲伐宗、脍、胥敖，南面而不释然，其故何也？"

Of yore, Mound asked Hibiscus: "I would send forces to punish Root, Mince, and Roam. When at court, I don't feel released. Why?"

舜曰："夫三子者，犹存乎蓬艾之间。若不释然，何哉？昔者十日并出，万物皆照，而况德之进乎日者乎？"

Hibiscus answered: "The three states are small ones like those in bushes. Why don't you feel released? Of yore, ten suns came out to shine upon all. Now, the light of your virtue is even stronger than sunlight."

啮缺问于王倪曰："子知物之所同是乎？"曰："吾恶乎知之！""子知子之所不知邪？"曰："吾恶乎知之！"

Teethmissing asked Kingsign: "Do you know all things are the same?" Kingsign answered: "How can I know that?" "Do you know what you don't know?" "How do I know that?"

"嚣则物无知邪？"曰："吾恶乎知之！虽然，尝试言之。庸讵知吾所谓知之非不知邪？庸讵知吾所谓不知之非知邪？且吾尝试问乎女：民湿寝则腰疾偏死，鳍然乎哉？木处则惴栗恂惧，猿猴然乎哉？三者孰知正处？民食刍豢，麋鹿食荐，蝍蛆甘带，鸱鸦耆鼠，四者孰知正味？猿猵狙以为雌，麋与鹿交，鳍与鱼游。毛嫱丽姬，人之所美也；鱼见之深入，鸟见之高飞，麋鹿见之决骤。四者孰知天下之正色哉？自我观之，仁义之端，是非之途，樊然殽乱，吾恶能知其辩！"

"Then, is there no way to know things?" "How can I know that?All the same, let me talk about it. How do you know the 'knowing' I say is not 'not knowing'? How do you know the 'not knowing' I say is not 'knowing'? And let me ask you: Sleeping in dampness, one will suffer from a backache or hemislegia. Is it the same case with loaches? Having climbed up a tall tree, one trembles with fear. Is it the same case with monkeys? Men, loaches, monkeys, which of the three know what good dwelling is? Men eat meat, deer eat grass, millipedes eat small snakes, and owls eat mice. Which of the four know what good taste is? Monkeys take baboons to wife; elks go mates with deer; loaches swim with fish. Lady Wool and Courtesan Belle are regarded as rare beauties, but when fish see them they sink deep, when birds see them they fly high, and when deer see them they flee fast. Which of the four know what real beauty is? As far as I can see, humanity or righteousness leads to disputes and chaos. How can I know their differences?"

齧缺曰：“子不知利害，则至人固不知利害乎？”王倪曰：“至人神矣！大泽焚而不能热，河汉冱而不能寒，疾雷破山、风振海而不能惊。若然者，乘云气，骑日月，而游乎四海之外，死生无变于己，而况利害之端乎！”

Teethmissing asked: “If you don’t know what good or harm is, don’t saints know that?” Kingsign answered: “A saint is mysterious! A forest on fire, he doesn’t feel hot; a river frozen, he doesn’t feel cold; a thunder breaking a hill, a gale shaking the sea, he is not frightened. So at ease, he rides a cloud, cruising the sun and the moon and touring the four seas. Death or life does not affect him, let alone the notion of good or harm!”

瞿鹊子问乎长梧子曰：“吾闻诸夫子：‘圣人不从事于务，不就利，不违害，不喜求，不缘道，无谓有谓，有谓无谓，而游乎尘垢之外。’夫子以为孟浪之言，而我以为妙道之行也。吾子以为奚若？”

Sir Magpie Halberd asked Sir Tall Tree: “I once heard Confucius say saints do not deal with worldly affairs, not caring for interests, not evading harms, not seeking felicity and not sticking to the Word, saying though not saying, not saying though saying, strolling out of dust. What Confucius regarded as rash I regard as subtle. What do you think?”

长梧子曰：“是黄帝之所听荧也，而丘也何足以知之！且女亦大早计，见卵而求时夜，见弹而求鸮炙。予尝为女妄言之，女以妄听之。奚旁日月，挟宇宙，为其吻合，置其滑涽，以隶相尊？众人役役，圣人愚芚，参万岁而一成纯。万物尽然，而以是相蕴。予恶乎知说生之非惑邪！予恶乎知恶死之非弱丧而不知归者邪！丽之姬，艾封人之子也，晋国之始得之也，涕泣沾襟；及其至于王所，与王同筐床，食刍豢，而后悔其泣也。予恶乎知夫死者不悔其始之蕲生乎！梦饮酒者，旦而哭泣；梦哭泣者，旦而田猎。方其梦也，不知其梦也。梦之中又占其梦焉，觉而后知其梦也。且有大觉而后知此其大梦也。而愚者自以为觉，窃窃然知之。君乎，牧乎，固哉！丘也与女，皆梦也；予谓女梦，亦梦也。是其言也，其名为吊诡。万世之后而一遇大圣，知其解者，是旦暮遇之也。”

Sir Tall Tree replied: “Even Lord Yellow would feel puzzled when hearing this. How could Confucius understand that? You are a little bit too hasty. Seeing an egg, you expect a rooster; seeing a pill, you expect a roast. Now, may I just say it and you just listen? Why not lean on the moon or the sun and hug the universe? Merge with all, leave troubles alone and be identified with all those low or high. The masses contend much while the saints look foolish, simplifying the havoc of all ages. Everything is like this, contained in pure chastity.” How do I know yearning to live is not an illusion? How do I know hating to die is not like wandering in an alien land and not knowing coming back home? Belle, a daughter of Wormwood’s guarding general, when captured by Chin’s army, cried all her lappet wet. When she lived in a palace in Chin, sleeping in the same bed with the king and eating delicacies, she regretted that she had cried. How do I not know those dead do not regret that they have yearned to live? The one who dreams of drinking liquor cries in the morning; the one who dreams of crying goes hunting in the morning. When one is dreaming, he does not know that he is dreaming. In a dream he may divine for a dream and knows it’s a dream when he wakes up. He finds it’s a big dream when he’s widely awake. A fool thinks he’s awake and thinks he knows everything. Lord or subject, how shallow it is! Confucius and you are both having a dream. When I say you are having a dream, I am also having a dream. What I have said now can be called a paradox. In an aeon from now, if one can come across a great saint, who can solve the puzzle, he’s the one you meet once in a blue moon.”

既使我与若辩矣，若胜我，我不若胜，若果是也，我果非也邪？我胜若，若不吾胜，我果是也，而果非也邪？其或是也，其或非也邪？其俱是也，其俱非也邪？我与若不能相知也，则人固受其黮暗，吾谁使正之？使同乎若者正之，既与若同矣，恶能正之！使同乎我者正之，既同乎我矣，恶能正之！使异乎我与若者正之，既异乎我与若矣，恶能正之！使同乎我与若者正之，既同乎我与若矣，恶能正之？然则我与若与人俱不能相知也，而待彼也邪？何谓和之以天倪？曰：是不是，然不然。是若果是也，则是之异乎不是也，亦无辩；然若果然也，则然之异乎不然也，亦无辩。化声之相待，若其不相待，和之以天倪，因之以曼衍，所以穷年也。忘年忘义，振于无竟，故寓诸无竟。

If you win and I lose when I debate with you, does it really mean that you are right and I am wrong? If I win and you lose, does it really mean that I am right and you are wrong? Is it that one is right and the other is wrong? Is it that we are both right or both wrong? Neither you nor I know, and all people are actually bound to ignorance. Who can we ask to make sound judgment? Ask the one who's similar to you? If he's similar to you, he can't make it! Ask the one who's similar to me? If he's similar to me, he can't make it! Ask the one who's different from you and me? If he's different from you and me, he can't make it! Ask the one who's similar to you and me? If he's similar to you and me, he can't make it. In that case, you, I and all others have no way to know, who else can we expect? A debate is like the opposition of forces in the change of sound, as if there's no opposition. It can but be attuned with natural forces to last until the end of life. What does it mean by attuned with natural forces? Aye goes with nay; truth goes with falsity. If aye is really aye, it is different from nay, then there's no room for debate; if truth is really truth, it is different from falsity, then there's no room for debate. Forget life or death, forget right or wrong, merge with infinitude, so all exist in infinitude.

罔两问景曰："曩子行，今子止；曩子坐，今子起；何其无特操与？"

The shade asked the shadow: "Now you walk, then you sit; now you sit, then you rise. Why are you so capricious?"

景曰："吾有待而然者邪？吾所待又有待而然者邪？吾待蛇蚹蜩翼邪？恶识所以然？恶识所以不然？"

The shadow replied: “Am I like that because I rely on something? Is what I rely on like that because it relies on something? Is what I rely on like the abdomen of a snake or the wings of a cicada? How can I know why I am like that? How can I know why I am not like that?”

昔者庄周梦为胡蝶，栩栩然胡蝶也。自喻适志与，不知周也。俄然觉，则蘧蘧然周也。不知周之梦为胡蝶与，胡蝶之梦为周与？周与胡蝶，则必有分矣。此之谓物化。

Once, Sir Lush dreamed that he transformed into a butterfly, a butterfly that flied so free, so carefree! It didn’t know it was Lush. Suddenly, he woke up and, in a surprise, realized that he was Lush. Did Lush dream of being a butterfly or a butterfly of being Lush? There must be a demarcation between Lush and the butterfly. This is what is called metamorphosis.

3. 养生主第三 Chapter Ⅲ: Sustaining Life

吾生也有涯，而知也无涯。以有涯随无涯，殆已！已而为知者，殆而已矣！为善无近名，为恶无近刑；缘督以为经，可以保身，可以全生，可以养亲，可以尽年。

Life is limited while knowledge is not. To follow the unlimited with the limited, one fails. As one has pursued knowledge, so he has failed. Do what is regarded as good, away from fame; do what is regarded as harm, free of penalty. Following the course of nature, one can sustain his life, maintain his nature, build up his body and enjoy a long life.

庖丁为文惠君解牛，手之所触，肩之所倚，足之所履，膝之所踦，砉然向然，奏刀騞然，莫不中音。合于《桑林》之舞，乃中《经首》之会。

A chef severed a carcass for Lord Lettergood. Where his hand touched, where his shoulder leaned, where his foot trod, and where his knee bent, there arose a whir, a clap, and his knife gave off a chop-chop, all concerted, in tune with the dance of *Mulberry Wood* and in accordance with the canto of *Straight Head*.

文惠君曰：“譆，善哉！技盖至此乎？”

Lord Lettergood exclaimed: “Wow, great! What a perfect skill!”

庖丁释刀对曰：“臣之所好者道也，进乎技矣。始臣之解牛之时，所见无非牛者；三年之后，未尝见全牛也。方今之时，臣以神遇而不以目视，官知止而神欲行。依乎天理，批大郤，导大窾，因其固然，技经肯綮之未尝，而况大軱乎！良庖岁更刀，割也；族庖月更刀，折也。今臣之刀十九年矣，所解数千牛矣，而刀刃若新发于硎。彼节者有间，而刀刃者无厚，以无厚入有间，恢恢乎其于游刃必有馀地矣。是以十九年而刀刃若新发于硎。虽然，每至于族，吾见其难为，怵然为戒，视为止，行为迟，动刀甚微。謋然已解，如土委地。提刀而立，为之四顾，为之踌躇满志，善刀而藏之。”

Laying down his knife, the chef replied: “What I love is the Word, beyond skills. When I first severed a carcass, what I saw was but a whole head of cattle. Three years later, I no longer saw the whole. And today I use my mind instead of my eyes, with no work of my organs but the operation of my soul. Based on the tissues of the carcass, I thrust my knife into the crevice between muscles or tendons and into the fissure amid joints, all in the nature of things. I never touch the the dense mesh of meridians and collaterals, let alone big bones. A good chef changes his knife in a year because he cuts; an ordinary chef changes his knife in a month because he hacks. Now I have used my knife for nineteen years, having severed thousands of carcasses. The blade is sharp as if newly honed. Joints have crevices while a blade shows no thickness. No thickness into crevices, there’s far more than enough room for my blade to go through. That’s why the knife I’ve used for nineteen years is still sharp as if newly honed. All the same, when I feel the density of fascia not easy to cut, I am all attention, a steady look, a slow motion, and a gentle sway of knife. All of a sudden, the carcass falls apart, like dust falling to the ground. Knife in hand, I stand and look around, feeling so satisfied. Then I clean my knife and store it away."

文惠君曰："善哉！吾闻庖丁之言，得养生焉。"

Lord Lettergood exclaimed: "Great! As I've heard what the chef said, I know how to keep fit."

公文轩见右师而惊曰："是何人也？恶乎介也？天与，其人与？"曰："天也，非人也。天之生是使独也，人之貌有与也。以是知其天也，非人也。"

When Letter Cart saw Right Master, he was so surprised: "What human is he? Why just one foot? Was he born like that or did he lose a foot?" He replied to himself: "He was born like that, not maimed. He was born with one foot. How one looks depends on Heaven. So I know it's Heaven, not human."

泽雉十步一啄，百步一饮，不蕲畜乎樊中。神虽王，不善也。

A pheasant in the marsh gets one peck in ten steps and one sip in a hundred, but it does not want to be caged. The bird in a cage looks vigorous, but not free.

老聃死，秦失吊之，三号而出。弟子曰："非夫子之友邪？"曰："然。""然则吊焉若此可乎？"曰："然。始也吾以为其人也，而今非也。向吾入而吊焉有老者哭之如哭其子；少者哭之如哭其母。彼其所以会之，必有不蕲言而言，不蕲哭而哭者。是遁天倍情，忘其所受，古者谓之遁天之刑。适来，夫子时也；适去，夫子顺也。安时而处顺，哀乐不能入也，古者谓是帝之县解。"

When Laocius died, Loss Ch'in paid a condolence call. He gave off but a few cries before he came out. One of his disciples asked: "Aren't you his friend?" "Yes." "Is it proper to mourn like that?" "Yes, before, I thought he was saintly; now I don't think it's true. When I went in to mourn, I found oldsters crying as if he was their son; I found youngsters crying as if he was their father.

They cried so sadly. They shouldn't have done that, saying like that, crying like that. It is against nature and they've forgotten the endowed span of life. It was called evasion of heavenly penalty in ancient times. In due time, you come; in due time, you go. If one's reassured in time and space, sadness or gladness will not affect him. It was called God's Redemption in ancient times."

指穷于为薪，火传也，不知其尽也。

A candle will burn out, but the use of fire is unlimited.

第六章　墨家
Chapter VI　Inkism

第一节　《墨子·兼爱》
Section 1　*Loving Others · Sir Ink*

1. 兼爱上 Loving Others (Upper)

若使天下兼相爱，爱人若爱其身，犹有不孝者乎？视父兄与君若其身，恶施不孝？犹有不慈者乎？视弟子与臣若其身，恶施不慈？故不孝不慈亡有。犹有盗贼乎？故视人之室若其室，谁窃？视人身若其身，谁贼？故盗贼亡有。犹有大夫之相乱家、诸侯之相攻国者乎？视人家若其家，谁乱？视人国若其国，谁攻？故大夫之相乱家，诸侯之相攻国者亡有。若使天下兼相爱，国与国不相攻，家与家不相乱，盗贼无有，君臣父子皆能孝慈，若此则天下治。故圣人以治天下为事者，恶得不禁恶而劝爱？故天下兼相爱则治，交相恶则乱。故子墨子曰：不可以不劝爱人者，此也。

Loving as loved in the world, loving others as loving oneself, will anyone not be filial? If treating his father, brothers, his lord as he treats himself, will he do anything unworthy or heartless? If one does nothing unworthy or heartless, will there be robbers or burglars? If one sees others' homes as his, why will he steal? If one protects others' bodies as he protects his own, why will he harm others? If there were no robbers or burglars, would lords and peers have to fight against each other? If one sees others' states as his own, will he have to wage wars? If one could love the other, no peers fighting, no lords attacking, no thieves stealing, lords loving subjects and fathers loving children, that would be a perfect world. Therefore, what else can a sage preoccupied with good governance do but to replace hatred with love? Love will lead to good governance and hatred chaos, and that's why Sir Ink said, "Do not stop the advocacy of loving others".

2. 兼爱中 Loving Others (Middle)

既以非之，何以易之？子墨子言曰：以兼相爱、交相利之法易之。然则兼相爱、交相利之法将奈何哉？子墨子言：视人之国若视其国，视人之家若视其家，视人之身若视其身。是故诸侯相爱则不野战，家主相爱则不相篡，人与人相爱则不相贼，君臣相爱则惠忠，父子相爱则慈孝，兄弟相爱则和调。天下之人皆相爱，强不执弱，众不劫寡，富不侮贫，贵不敖贱，诈不欺愚。

Knowing that not loving is wrong, how can we change it? Sir Ink said: "Change by making people love and benefit each other." But how can we make people love and benefit each other? Sir Ink said: See others' states as one's own; see others' families as one's own; see others' bodies as one's own. Thus kings loving each other, there will be no wars; families loving each other, there will be no plunders; people loving each other, there will be no mutual harm; emperor and ministers loving each other, there will be benevolence and loyalty; fathers and sons loving each other, there will be affection and piety; brothers loving each other, there will be harmony. People in the world loving each other, the strong will not manipulate the weak, the many will not force the few, the wealthy will not bully the poor, the noble will not humiliate the low, and the crafty will not cheat the dumb.

夫爱人者，人亦从而爱之；利人者，人亦从而利之；恶人者，人亦从而恶之；害人者，人亦从而害之。

He who loves others will be loved by others; he who benefits others will benefited by others; he who hates others will be hated by others; he who harms others will be harmed by others.

3. 兼爱下 Loving Others (Lower)

仁人之事者，必务求兴天下之利，除天下之害。

A benevolent man is committed to prospering the world and ridding the world of harms.

第二节 《墨子·尚贤》
Section 2 *Respecting Sages* · *Sir Ink*

1. 尚贤上 Respecting Sages (Upper)

子墨子言曰：今者王公大人为政于国家者，皆欲国家之富，人民之众，刑政之治。然而不得富而得贫，不得众而得寡，不得治而得乱，则是本失其所欲，得其所恶。是其故何也？子墨子言曰：是在王公大人为政于国家者，不能以尚贤事能为政也。是故国有贤良之士众，则国家之治厚；贤良之士寡，则国家之治薄。故大人之务，将在于众贤而已。

Sir Ink said: “Now lords and ministers administer to prosper the state, increase the population and make public affairs in order, but the result is poverty instead of prosperity, decreased population instead of increased one, and disorder instead of order. Why do they lose what they hope for and get what they detest?” He answered himself: “That is because they can’t respect the noble and use the able. In a state, if there are plenty of men noble or able, the state will achieve a lot, but if there are few, the state will achieve very little. So a lord needs to gather more noble men.”

故官无常贵，而民无终贱，有能则举之，无能则下之，举公义，辟私怨，此若言之谓也。

(Thus) neither the humility of people is eternal, nor is the honor of officials. The talented can be promoted, and the incompetent can be dismissed. Just as what Sir Ink said, so justice is promulgated and hidden resentment is avoided.

是故国有贤良之士众，则国家之治厚；贤良之士寡，则国家之治薄。故大人之务，将在于众贤而已。

If a country has many talents, there will be greater governance; if a country has few talents, there will be less successful governance. Therefore, the main task of a ruler is to gather talents.

故得士则谋不困，体不劳，名立而功成，美章而恶不生，则由得士也。

With talents, schemes will not be difficult to be made, and the body will not be exhausted, achievements could be made, virtues could be highlighted, and evils could be curbed. This is the function of talents.

2. 尚贤中 Respecting Sages (Middle)

听其言，迹其行，察其所能，而慎予官。

Listen to his words and observe his deeds and appoint him carefully according to his competence.

不辨贫富、贵贱、远迩、亲疏，贤者举而尚之，不肖者抑而废之。

A virtuous man should be recommended to hold a high office whether poor or rich, distinguished or humble, close or estranged, while the one without virtue should be restrained and removed from his office.

第三节 其他篇目
Section 3 Other Articles

1. 非攻 No War

国家发政，夺民之用，废民之利，若此甚众，然而何为为之？曰：我贪伐胜之名，及得之利，故为之。子墨子言曰：计其所自胜，无所可用也；计其所得，反不如所丧者之多。

It's common that states start wars, depriving the folks of their properties and destroying their livelihoods. Why do such things happen? The answer is: One does this to get both fame and benefits. Sir Ink said, what he wins is useless and he gains turns out to be less than what he has lost.

子墨子言曰：今天下之所誉善者，其说将何哉？为其上中天之利，而中中鬼之利，而下中人之利。

Sir Ink said: How can I say about what the world today praise? Above, this is in line with the law of Heaven; in the middle, it is in accordance with the law of ghosts; below, it can meet the requirements of people.

是故古之仁人有天下者，必反大国之说，一天下之和，总四海之内。焉率天下之百姓，以农臣事上帝山川鬼神。利人多，功故又大，是以天赏之，鬼富之，人誉之，使贵为天子，富有天下，名参乎天地，至今不废。此则知者之道也，先王之所以有天下者也。

That's why the good lords of yore objected to warfare among large states for the harmony and unity of all, so they encouraged all folks to farm and acted as servants to Heaven, hills and rills as well as ghosts and gods. They contributed a lot to people's well-being, so Heaven rewarded them, ghosts and gods enriched them and people praised them, so much so that they were honored as lords of the world and their names are remembered even today. This is precisely the Word of sages and this is why lords have the world.

夫杀之人，灭鬼神之主，废灭先王，贼虐万民，百姓离散，则此中不中鬼之利矣。意将以为利人乎？夫杀之人，为利人也博矣。又计其费，此为周生之本，竭天下百姓之财用，不可胜数也，则此下不中人之利矣。

Those killers kill the people who worship ghosts and gods, kill their kings and abuse their folks. If this is athwart the will of ghosts and gods, will this do good to the people? These killers actually get little from killing, instead they exhaust people's wealth, too much to count, which is also contrary to the benefit of the people.

2. 七患 Seven Dangers

子墨子曰：国有七患。七患者何？城郭沟池不可守，而治宫室，一患也；边国至境，四邻莫救，二患也；先尽民力无用之功，赏赐无能之人，民力尽于无用，财宝虚于待客，三患也；仕者持禄，游者爱佼，君修法讨臣，臣慑而不敢拂，四患也；君自以为圣智而不问事，自以为安强而无守备，四邻谋之不知戒，五患也；所信者不忠，所忠者不信，六患也；畜种菽粟不足以食之，大臣不足以事之，赏赐不能喜，诛罚不能威，七患也。以七患居国，必无社稷；以七患守城，敌至国倾。七患之所当，国必有殃。

Sir Ink said: There are seven dangers for a state. What are they? Number one, palaces are built while the town and moat cannot be defended. Number two, invaders approach while neighbors do not help. Number three, financial resources are exhausted on useless things and bestowed on good-for-nothings and money is squandered on guests. Number four, officials only occupy their posts while folks gather to tide over their worries. The lord revises laws to punish his subjects, who dare not protest. Number five, the lord regards himself as divine but does not fulfill his responsibility. The lord regards the state as stable and strong, hence no defense, unaware that neighbors will soon attack.

Number six, the dishonest are trusted, and the honest are spurned. Number seven, there is not enough food for people and livestock; senior officials do not do their part in state affairs. Awards cannot make people happy nor can punishments deter them. A state with these seven disasters are doomed to face catastrophes.

故时年岁善，则民仁且良；时年岁凶，则民吝且恶。夫民何常此之有？为者疾，食者众，则岁无丰。故曰：财不足则反之时，食不足则反之用。故先民以时生财，固本而用财，则财足。

A bumper year makes people kind and merciful while a lean year makes them mean and evil. One's nature is not fixed! When there are more people to feed than people to work, it cannot be a bumper year. It is time to reflect on farming when there is not enough wealth; it is time to reflect on spending when there is not enough food. Ancients made fortune in accordance with farming time. They cultivated hard and used money properly. As a result, they could live affluently.

食者国之宝也，兵者国之爪也，城者所以自守也，此三者国之具也。

Grains are a treasure, weapons tools, and city walls for defence. These three are what to sustain a state with.

3. 天志 Heaven's Will

然则天亦何欲何恶？天欲义而恶不义。然则率天下之百姓以从事于义，则我乃为天之所欲也。我为天之所欲，天亦为我所欲。然则我何欲何恶？我欲福禄而恶祸祟。若我不为天之所欲，而为天之所不欲，然则我率天下之百姓以从事于祸祟中也。然则何以知天之欲义而恶不义？曰：天下有义则生，无义则死；有义则富，无义则贫；有义则治，无义则乱，然则天欲其生而恶其死，欲其富而恶其贫，欲其治而恶其乱。此我所以知天欲义而恶不义也。

Then, what does Heaven love or hate? Heaven loves justice and hates injustice. Then, leading the masses in the world to do justice is what Heaven loves. If we do what Heaven loves, then Heaven will do what we love. Then, what do we love and what do we hate? We love bliss and hate curses. If we do not do what Heaven loves but do what Heaven does not love, then we are leading the masses in the world to curses. How do we know Heaven loves justice and hates injustice? The answer is: In the world what is justice exists and what is injustice perishes; what is justice will be rich and what is injustice will be poor; what is justice will be order and what is injustice will be chaos. In that case, Heaven loves humans to reproduce and hates them to die, loves them to be rich and hates them to be poor, loves them to be peaceful and hates them to be chaotic. This is how I know Heaven loves justice and hates injustice.

顺天意者，义政也；反天意者，力政也。然义政将奈何哉？子墨子言曰：处大国不攻小国，处大家不篡小家，强者不劫弱，贵者不傲贱，多诈者不欺愚。

Those who follow Heaven govern with justice, and those who disobey Heaven govern with force. What will just governance be? Sir Ink says, a big country as yours does not invade those small ones, a big clan as yours does not usurp those small ones, the strong does not coerce the weak, the superior does not bully the inferior, tricksters take no advantage of the less intelligent.

4. 尚同 Alignment with Superiors

必疾爱而使之，致信而持之，富贵以道其前，明罚以率其后。为政若此，唯欲毋与我同，将不可得也。

People can be worked if treated with sincere affection and can be won if trusted. They can be guided with affluence forward and supervised with punishments afterward. In this way, it's impossible to alienate the lord and his people.

5. 辞过 Criticism of Negligence

凡此五者，圣人之所俭节也，小人之所淫佚也。俭节则昌，淫佚则亡，此五者不可不节。夫妇节而天地和，风雨节而五谷孰，衣服节而肌肤和。

The five mentioned above can be summed up as saints' thrift and flunkies' extravagance. The thrifty will flourish, and the extravagant will perish. These five must be restrained. When a couple's affairs are good, Heaven and earth will be smooth, when wind and rain are good, there will be a good harvest, and when clothing is well prepared, the body will feel comfortable.

6. 节用 Saving

去无用之费，圣王之道，天下之大利也。

He is a wise king who saves unnecessary expenses, as is good for the people.

7. 亲士 Appointing Talents

入国而不存其士，则亡国矣。见贤而不急，则缓其君矣。非贤无急，非士无与虑国。缓贤忘士，而能以其国存者，未曾有也。

A state would perish if no able man enjoys precedence. An able man put aside, he will give a cold shoulder to the lord in return, so there is nothing more urgent than appointing able men. Nobody will plan state affairs without able men, and there is no former example for a state to enjoy long term stability with its able men neglected.

8. 修身 Character Cultivation

志不强者智不达，言不信者行不果。据财不能以分人者，不足与友；守道不笃、偏物不博、辩是非不察者，不足与游。本不固者未必几，雄而不修者其后必惰。

He who has no strong will is not high in intelligence; he who speaks without credit is not resolute in action; he who has wealth but refuses to give does not deserve to make friends; he who does not have a firm stand nor have extensive experience nor know how to distinguish between right and wrong does not deserve to keep company. If the root is not deep, the branches will wither; if one is brave but slack in moral cultivation, he will fail later.

名不可简而成也，誉不可巧而立也。

Reputation takes time to be; honor can't be gained with fraud.

9. 非乐 Prohibition of Music

民有三患：饥者不得食，寒者不得衣，劳者不得息。三者民之巨患也。

There are three worries for people: no food for the hungry, no clothes for the freezing, and no rest for the tired.

10. 贵义 Esteem for Righteousness

争一言以相杀，是贵义于其身也。故曰：万事莫贵于义也。

That people struggle against one another for a single principle indicates that righteousness is more valuable than their own lives. So nothing is more important than righteousness.

11. 耕柱 Sir Tillpillar

所为贵良宝者，可以利民也，而义可以利人。故曰：义，天下之良宝也。

Treasures and valuables benefit people, thus they are cherished. Righteousness benefits people, so righteousness is a valuable thing.

第七章 法家
Chapter VII Legalism

第一节 《韩非子·解老》
Section 1 *Expounding Laocius · Sir Hanfei*

1. 解老上 Expounding Laocius (Upper)

所谓廉者，必生死之命也，轻恬资财也。所谓直者，义必公正，公心不偏党也。所谓光者，官爵尊贵，衣裘壮丽也。今有道之士，虽中外信顺，不以诽谤穷堕；虽死节轻财，不以侮罢羞贪；虽义端不党，不以去邪罪私；虽势尊衣美，不以夸贱欺贫。其故何也？使失路者而肯听习问知，即不成迷也。今众人之所以欲成功而反为败者，生于不知道理而不肯问知而听能。众人不肯问知听能，而圣人强以其祸败适之，则怨。众人多而圣人寡，寡之不胜众，数也。今举动而与天下之为仇，非全身长生之道也，是以行轨节而举之也。故曰："方而不割，廉而不刿，直而不肆，光而不耀。"

Integrity refers to a character of disregarding one's own life and spurning property; justice refers to a conduct that one cares for the common good and never gangs up for selfish interest; brightness refers to peers and high ranking officials whose garments are gorgeous. Worthies at present win the public's trust at home and abroad, nevertheless, they do not slander those who are poor or low; they are willing to risk their lives and disregard property, but do not insult those deposed or humiliate those malfeasants; they are upright and refrain from involving in a clique for selfish interest, but they do not abandon those who are treacherous and selfish; they enjoy power and gorgeous garments, but do not show off in front of the poor nor bully them. Why? If one who has lost his way asks one who knows the way will not be a strayer. The reason why people fail is that they, unwilling to ask the able, do not know the way and wherefore. If they are unwilling to learn from the able, sages will blame them for their faults, and in return, they will complain. Average people are many, and sages few. Sages are hopelessly outnumbered. So to breed enmity with common people is not the way to keep safe and live long. Therefore, one'd better act with temperance, as is said, "the sage executes justice rather than roughness, rigor rather than harm, candor rather than lust, light rather than glare".

故以理观之：事大众而数摇之，则少成功；藏大器而数徙之，则多败伤；烹小鲜而数挠之，则贼其责；治大国而数变法，则民苦之。是以有道之君贵静，不重变法。故曰："治大国者若烹小鲜。"

Therefore, by reasoning I can see if tasks are big, many and frequently shifted, few of them can be accomplished; if anybody keeps a great vessel and moves it too often, it is prone to damages; when frying small fish, if you poke them around too often, you will ruin the fish; when you govern a big state, if you alter laws and decrees too often, people will suffer pains. Therefore, a ruler who follows the Word values tranquility and takes the alteration of law seriously. Hence Laocius's saying:"Ruling a large state is like cooking small fish."

2. 解老下 Expounding Laocius (Lower)

人有欲，则计会乱；计会乱，而有欲甚；有欲甚，则邪心胜；邪心胜，则事经绝；事经绝，则祸难生。由是观之，祸难生于邪心，邪心诱于可欲。可欲之类，进则教良民为奸，退则令善人有祸。奸起，则上侵弱君；祸至，则民人多伤。然则可欲之类，上侵弱君而下伤人民。夫上侵弱君而下伤人民者，大罪也。故曰："祸莫大于可欲。"是以圣人不引五色，不淫于声乐；明君贱玩好而去淫丽。

Lust disturbs a scheme; a disturbed scheme gives rise to more lust; more lust yields to the prevalence of evils; the prevalence of evils transgresses regulations, and transgressed regulations cause disasters. Hence, disasters arise from evil thoughts, and evil thoughts from avarice. What causes lust may turn good people onto evil ones or to say the least, cause them much trouble. Evils may weaken lords above; troubles arriving will harm the masses. So what causes lust to weaken lords and harm the masses is a great sin. As is said, "No bane is greater than greediness." Therefore, saints are not tempted by five colors or abandoned to pleasures of songs and women; divine lords ignore playthings and give up luxuries.

第二节　其他篇目
Section 2　Other Articles

1. 有度 Within a Limit

国无常强，无常弱。奉法者强，则国强；奉法者弱，则国弱。

No state is permanently strong; no state is permanently weak. If conformers to law are strong, a state will be strong; if conformers to law are weak, a state will be weak.

故以法治国，举措而已矣。法不阿贵，绳不挠曲。法之所加，智者弗能辞，勇者弗敢争。刑过不避大臣，赏善不遗匹夫。故矫上之失，诘下之邪，治乱决缪，绌羡齐非，一民之轨，莫如法。厉官威民，退淫殆，止诈伪，莫如刑。刑重，则不敢以贵易贱；法审，则上尊而不侵。上尊而不侵，则主强而守要，故先王贵之而传之。人主释法用私，则上下不别矣。

So ruling with law is nothing but getting it implemented. The law does not favor power, just like a gauge bends for none. Held liable, one cannot evade, wise or brave. A minister is no exception in case of punishment; a commoner should not be neglected if he's worth rewarding. Nothing is better than law when it comes to the rectification of misbehaving superiors, the punishment of erring inferiors, the restoration of order out of chaos, the correction of mistakes with rectitude, and the guidance of the people to norms. Nothing is better than punishment when it comes to the regulation of officials or the deterrence of the public, the ridding of promiscuity and indolence, and the prevention of fraud. Heavy penalties can stop high officials from disdaining lower ones, and strict laws can prevent a lord's honor from being undermined so that he can be strong and powerful. Therefore, our late king attached great importance to law and would like to see this tradition to be passed down. If a lord prefers personal considerations to the execution of law, nothing can set him apart from his inferiors or subjects.

2．诡使 Deviation from the Right Path

夫立法令者，以废私也。法令行而私道废矣。私者，所以乱法也。

Law is made to ban self-interest and self-interest will not exist if law is executed. Self-interest causes trouble.

故曰："道私者乱，道法者治。"

Therefore, the pursuit of self-interest leads to chaos; the observation of law leads to stability.

3．难势 Difficult Situations

抱法处势则治，背法去势则乱。

Law and trend followed, order obtains; law or trend thwarted, chaos arises.

4．说疑 Explaining Doubts

故有道之主，远仁义，去智能，服之以法。是以誉广而名威，民治而国安，知用民之法也。凡术也者，主之所执也；法也者，官之所师也。

Therefore, a lord pursuing the right path abandons benevolence and righteousness, discards wisdom and ability, and subdues people by means of law. That being so, his fame spreads far and wide, his name becomes awe inspiring, his subjects are orderly, and his country safe, because he knows how to employ people. As a rule, tactics is what a lord holds in hand; law is what officials take as models.

5. 内储说上七术 Seven Methods to Manage Subjects

爱多者则法不立；威寡者则下侵上。是以刑罚不必则禁令不行。

If a lord is too kind, law will not stand; if his authority is too weak, inferiors will offend superiors. Therefore, if penalties are not definite, prohibitions or decrees will not be effective.

子产相郑，病将死，谓游吉曰："我死后，子必用郑，必以严莅人。夫火形严，故人鲜灼；水形懦，人多溺。子必严子之形，无令溺子之懦。"

When Sir Production (Tsuch'an), Premier of Cheng, was ill and dying, he told Yuchi: "After my death you will certainly be appointed by Cheng. Be sure to manage people with severity. Fire appears severe, but people rarely get burned; water appears mild, but people often get drowned. You must make your penalties severe and do not let people commit crime because of your kindness."

6. 五蠹 Five Types of Assholes

是以圣人不期修古，不法常可，论世之事，因为之备。

Therefore, sages do not seek to follow the ways of ancients or establish standards for all ages but examine things at the time and deal with them.

7. 八经 Eight Eternal Rites

凡治天下，必因人情。人情者，有好恶，故赏罚可用；赏罚可用，则禁令可立而治道具矣。

Any one who governs the world must consider human feelings. Feelings can be good or bad, so reward or punishment can be employed. If reward or punishment is properly employed and injunctions are effective, all regulations will be widely binding and acceptable.

8. 南面 Reigning

主道者，使人臣有必言之责，又有不言之责。言无端末辩无所验者，此言之责也；以不言避责持重位者，此不言之责也。人主使人臣言者必知其端以责其实，不言者必问其取舍以为之责，则人臣莫敢妄言矣，又不敢默然矣，言、默则皆有责也。

The right way to reign is to make all ministers understand why they are blamed for giving opinions and why they are blamed for not giving opinions. If they utter words without beginning or ending or have an argument that has no proof, then they are blamed for giving opinions; if they attempt to evade responsibilities by not giving any opinion so as to maintain their high status, then they are blamed for not giving opinions. A lord in keeping ministers in service ought to know the motive of every speaker in order to hold his words responsible for an equivalent fact, and ask non-speakers to decide between the pros and cons of the propositions so as to hold them accountable for their work. So, nobody will dare to give an arbitrary opinion or keep silent. Because both speaking and silence equally involve accountabilities.

9. 人主 Political Life

明主者，推功而爵禄，称能而官事，所举者必有贤，所用者必有能，贤能之士进，则私门之请止矣。

A sage lord respects a person with meritorious performance, confers a title of nobility and offers salaries to him, appoints him to an official position after weighing his capabilities. Those who are recommended must be virtuous; those who are recruited must be talented. Since those virtuous and talented ones are recruited in the court, the trend of seeking official positions by personal relationship or bribery will be curbed naturally.

10. 扬权 Enhancing Monarchial Power

夫物者有所宜，材者有所施，各处其宜，故上下无为。使鸡司夜，令狸执鼠，皆用其能，上乃无事。上有所长，事乃不方。矜而好能，下之所欺；辩惠好生，下因其材。上下易用，国故不治。

Things have their uses, advantages and proper places, so there is no fuss up and down. Let the rooster do its morning call and let the cat catch mice. Each is used properly, and no trouble arises. If a monarch shows his talent, he will fail as a king; if a monarch likes to brag, his subjects will cheat; if he likes to show off his eloquence or intelligence, he will be taken advantage of. If a head is used as a tail, a state cannot be governed well.

11. 亡征 Signs of a Dying Nation

缓心而无成，柔茹而寡断，好恶无决而无所定立者，可亡也。

He who acts hesitantly is bound to fail; he who is indecisive, uncritical and undecided will perish.

恃交援而简近邻，怙强大之救而侮所迫之国者，可亡也。羁旅侨士，重帑在外，上间谋计，下与民事者，可亡也。民信其相，下不能其上，主爱信之而弗能废者，可亡也。境内之杰不事，而求封外之士，不以功伐课试，而好以名问举错，羁旅起贵以陵故常者，可亡也。大心而无悔，国乱而自多，不料境内之资而易其邻敌者，可亡也。国小而不处卑，力少而不畏强，无礼而侮大邻，贪愎而拙交者，可亡也。

Those states are prone to perish that rely on alliances while ignoring neighbors and count on supports from big powers while bullying other states.

Those states are prone to perish where foreign residents invest large sums of money and interfere in national secrets and local people's welfare. Those states are prone to perish where people trust prime ministers but disobey the lord or the lord favors the prime minister, unable to depose him. Those states are prone to perish where domestic talents are not used but alien talents are sought, where one's merit is not judged by the performance but by name and family background and where alien residents are promoted to overpower domestic ones...Those states are prone to perish where the lord is self-important without repentance, self-praising though in trouble and neglecting opponents irrespective of his own strength. Those states are prone to perish that are small but arrogant, weak but fearless, impolite and insulting powerful neighbors, greedy, stubborn and ignorant of diplomacy.

12. 显学 Famous Learning

观容服，听辞言，仲尼不能以必士；试之官职，课其功伐，则庸人不疑于愚智。

Given only outfits or remarks, even Confucius cannot tell whether one can be an official; checking officials with their positions and looking into their achievements, even a mediocre man can tell a fool from a sage.

明主举实事，去无用。

Wise lords go for practicality instead of vanity.

征赋钱粟以实仓库，且以救饥馑、备军旅也。

Plenty of money and grain should be collected to replenish the national treasury against a famine or war.

13. 用人 Employing People

治国之臣，效功于国以履位，见能于官以受职，尽力于权衡以任事。

Only when one makes great contribution to his country can he become a minister; only when his competence is shown at work can he fit the position; only when he does his best to take charge can he manage great affairs.

14. 大体 Overall Situation

利莫长于简，福莫久于安。

There is no benefit better than frugality, and there is no fortune longer than stability.

15. 主道 The Way to Reign

是故明君之行赏也，暧乎如时雨，百姓利其泽；其行罚也，畏乎如雷霆，神圣不能解也。故明君无偷赏，无赦罚。赏偷，则功臣堕其业；赦罚，则奸臣易为非。是故诚有功，则虽疏贱必赏；诚有过，则虽近爱必诛。疏贱必赏，近爱必诛，则疏贱者不怠，而近爱者不骄也。

Therefore, in terms of a lord's reward or punishment, his grace is as mild as the rain that nourishes all, and his punishment as terrible as thunder that even a deity cannot evade. Therefore, an lord does not give or forgive at random. A meritorious officer may slacken if a reward is given at random, and a traitor is apt to swagger when he is pardoned. Therefore, if meritorious enough, one will be rewarded no matter how far away or lowly he is; if guilty indeed, one will be punished even if he is a close relative or is much loved. With a strict system of rewarding and punishment, even those far away or lowly will not slacken, and even those close or loved will not be arrogant.

16. 奸劫弑臣 Treacherous, Coercive, and Murderous Officials

夫有施与贫困，则无功者得赏；不忍诛罚，则暴乱者不止。

If he helps the poor, an idler may get the help; if he does not bear to kill or punish, rebels and rioters arise.

第八章　兵家
Chapter VIII　Military Strategy

第一节　《孙子兵法》
Section 1　*Wu Sun's Art of War*

1. 始计 Planning

兵者，国之大事，死生之地，存亡之道，不可不察也。

War, a great matter of the state, a matter of life or death, existence or subjugation, must be investigated.

道者，令民与上同意也，故可以与之死，可以与之生，而不畏危。

The Word can harmonize inferiors with superiors, so that they can die or live with it without fear.

将者，智、信、仁、勇、严也。

A general is one who is resourceful, faithful, benevolent, brave and strict.

夫未战而庙算胜者，得算多也；未战而庙算不胜者，得算少也。多算胜，少算不胜，而况于无算乎！吾以此观之，胜负见矣。

Not yet in war he calculates he will win, because there are many conditions for that; not yet in war he calculates he will not win because there are few conditions for that. If you have many conditions, you win, and if you have few, you won't, let alone you don't have any. From this, I can see that winning or losing can be predicted.

2. 谋攻 Strategy

孙子曰：凡用兵之法：全国为上，破国次之；全军为上，破军次之；全旅为上，破旅次之；全卒为上，破卒次之；全伍为上，破伍次之。是故百战百胜，非善之善者也；不战而屈人之兵，善之善者也。

Suncius said: "For all the art of war, conquering the whole state is the best and destroying it the next; similarly, conquering the whole army is the best and destroying it the next; conquering the whole brigade is the best and destroying it the next; conquering the whole squad is the best and destroying it the next; conquering the whole quintuplet is the best and destroying it the next. Thus, winning all wars is not the best of the best, subduing the enemy without fighting is."

故上兵伐谋，其次伐交，其次伐兵，其下攻城。攻城之法，为不得已。

Therefore, the best way is scheming to win, the next, using diplomacy, the next further, using forces, and the last storming the town. The storming of a town is the last resort to take.

修橹轒辒，具器械，三月而后成；距闉，又三月而后已。将不胜其忿而蚁附之，杀士三分之一，而城不拔者，此攻之灾也。故善用兵者，屈人之兵而非战也，拔人之城而非攻也，毁人之国而非久也，必以全争于天下，故兵不顿而利可全，此谋攻之法也。

It takes three months to make shields and war wagons, and prepare tools, and another three months to build forts. It is the harm of attacking a city if a general, frustrated and irritated, drives his soldiers like ants but the city is not yet taken when one third of the troops are killed. Thus, a good commander subdues enemy without engaging field battles, captures cities without swarm attacks and conquers enemy states without lengthy wars.

故兵不顿而利可全，此谋攻之法也。

He must win the world with full success. So, winning the war without crippling his own army is the principle of war.

故知胜有五：知可以战与不可以战者胜，识众寡之用者胜，上下同欲者胜，以虞待不虞者胜，将能而君不御者胜。

Therefore, we can foresee five kinds of victory: if one can judge whether a battle can be fought or not, he wins; if well equipped with forces according to the enemy and himself, he wins; if his army work well up and down, he wins; if well prepared against the unprepared, he wins; if able to command without his lord's constraint, he wins.

知彼知己者，百战不殆；不知彼而知己，一胜一负；不知彼不知己，每战必败。

If you know the other and yourself, you will never lose; if you do not know the other but yourself, you may win or lose; if you know neither the other nor yourself, you will lose every battle you fight.

3. 九变 Nine Changes

故用兵之法，无恃其不来，恃吾有以待也；无恃其不攻，恃吾有所不可攻也。

Therefore, the art of war teaches us we should not place hopes on no happening of war but make good preparation, and should not place hopes on no launch of attacks but be ready to form impregnable defence.

4. 行军 Marching

兵非益多也，惟无武进，足以并力、料敌、取人而已。夫惟无虑而易敌者，必擒于人。卒未亲附而罚之，则不服，不服，则难用也；卒已亲附而罚不行，则不可用也。故令之以文，齐之以武，是谓必取。令素行以教其民，则民服；令不素行以教其民，则民不服。令素行者，与众相得也。

What matters is not how many soldiers you have. No rash move but concentration of forces, estimation of the enemy and appointment of a good commander. He who exercises no forethought but slights his opponents is sure to be captured. Soldiers will not be submissive if they are punished before they are close to you; unless submissive, they are practically useless. If soldiers are close to you but there is no enforcement of punishments, they will still be unless. Therefore, soldiers must be treated in the first instance with humanity, but kept under control by means of iron discipline, as is the certain road to victory. If in training soldiers commands are habitually enforced, the army will be well-disciplined; if not, its discipline will be loose. If a general insists on his orders being obeyed, the gain will be mutual.

5. 九地 Nine Places

将军之事，静以幽，正以治。

A general needs to be quiet, hence secrecy and upright, hence order.

6. 军争 Military Scramble

故三军可夺气，将军可夺心。

An army may be robbed of its spirit; a commander may be robbed of his mind.

7. 地形 Topography

夫地形者，兵之助也。料敌制胜，计险厄远近，上将之道也。知此而用战者必胜，不知此而用战者必败。故战道必胜，主曰无战，必战可也；战道不胜，主曰必战，无战可也。故进不求名，退不避罪，唯人是保，而利合于主，国之宝也。

Terrains can be of help in wars. Judge the enemy to win the war, and check whether the terrains are steep or even, near or far, as is a principle for wise commanders. Those knowing it in a war will win; those not knowing it in a war will lose. Thus, if the principle guarantees winning, launch the war, even if the lord disagrees; if there is no guarantee, don't start a war, even if the lord agrees. So, advance not to gain fame, withdraw not to dodge duties; act only to protect people and benefit the lord. Such commanders are the treasure of a state.

第二节 《孙膑兵法》
Section 2 *Pin Sun's Art of War*

1. 篡卒 Picking of Valiant Soldiers

孙子曰：兵之胜在于篡卒，其勇在于制，其巧在于势，其利在于信，其德在于道，其富在于亟归，其强在于休民，其伤在于数战。

Pin Sun said: "Victories depend on the picking of valiant soldiers; valorous troops depend on the system; ingenious tactics depend on the advantage; the strength of troops depends on faith; the virtue of troops depends on the Word; the effectiveness of troops depends on the timely end of a war; the power of troops depends on recuperation; the enervation of troops is due to endless fighting."

2. 行篡 Select Worthies

孙子曰：用兵移民之道，权衡也。权衡，所以篡贤取良也。阴阳，所以聚众合敌也。正衡再纍……既忠，是谓不穷。称乡县衡，虽其宜也。私公之财壹也。

Pin Sun said: "One must weigh the pros and cons when recruiting soldiers for a war. Weighing is the means to select worthies and talents while Shade and Shine is something used to build up forces. Weigh it up so that talents spring up without end; weigh it up again and again just for proper results. Private and public properties must be used for the same purpose".

3. 见威王 An Audience with King Power

夫兵者，非士恒势也。此先王之傅道也。战胜，则所以在亡国而继绝世也。战不胜，则所以削地而危社稷也。是故兵者不可不察。然夫乐兵者亡，而利胜者辱。兵非所乐也，而胜非所利也。事备而后动。故城小而守固者，有委也；卒寡而兵强者，有义也。夫守而无委，战而无义，天下无能以固且强者。

War is never certain, as has been taught by ancient lords. A victory can rescue a perishing country and an endangered race; a defeat will cost a territory and endanger the safety of the state. Therefore, war is something that one can never neglect. Bellicose rulers will perish, and generals coveting victory will incur shame. War is not a plaything, and a victory is not a gain. Preparation precedes an operation. Therefore, a small town can be well fortified with provisions and a small number of soldiers can be forceful with justice. Nobody in the world can be both fortified and forceful if having no provisions or fighting an unjust war.

4. 八阵 Eight Battle Formations

夫安万乘国，广万乘王，全万乘之民命者，唯知道。知道者，上知天之道，下知地之理，内得其民之心，外知敌之情，阵则知八阵之经，见胜而战，弗见而诤，此王者之将也。

It is the Word of war that a general must know to consolidate the power of a large state, to strengthen the safety of his lord, and to protect people's life and property. A general is considered knowing the Word of war if he knows the Word of Heaven and the way of earth, has the support of the public, understands the enemy's situation, knows various kinds of army formations, fights only when he's sure to win, and fights not when he's not sure. Such a general is the one who can assist the lord.

第三节《兵经·肃》
Section 3 *Solemnity · Canons for War*

号令一发三军威慑，鼓进金止，炮起铃食，飒奋麾驰。雨不避舍，热不释甲，劳不弃械，见难不退，遇利不取，陷城不妄杀，有功不骄伐，趋行不闻声，冲之不动，震之不惊，掩之不奔，截之不分，是为肃。

The army thunder at an order: hearing a drum they march; hearing a gong, they stop; hearing a cannon, they set off; hearing a bell, they dine; seeing a command flag, they stride ahead. Though it rains, they do not take shelter; though it is hot, they do not doff their armors; though tired, they do not discard their weapons. Further, in difficulties, they do not flinch; facing interest, they do not scramble. They do not slay when having conquered a city, do not boast when having won a battle and do not make sound when marching. They stand firm when offended, keep calm in case of emergency, stay put when attacked, and remain together when intercepted. Such is discipline.

第四节　《吴子·图国》
Section 4 *Governing the State · Ch'i Wu*

凡兵之所起者有五：一曰争名，二曰争利，三曰积恶，四曰内乱，五曰因饥。其名又有五：一曰义兵，二曰强兵，三曰刚兵，四曰暴兵，五曰逆兵。禁暴救乱曰义，恃众以伐曰强，因怒兴师曰刚，弃礼贪利曰暴，国乱人疲，举事动众曰逆。五者之服，各有其道，义必以礼服，强必以谦服，刚必以辞服，暴必以诈服，逆必以权服。

In general, there are five causes for a war: fame, profits, increased feud, civil strife, and famines. And there are five types of war: just war, overbearing war, inflamed war, looting war, and perverse war. Just, because it is to check violence and remove chaos; overbearing, because it is punitive by strong force; inflamed, because it is due to the anger of the lord; looting, because it is aimed at trophies; perverse, because it is waged out of the state's chaos and exhaustion. There are respective measures to the five kinds of war: reasoning versus the just, humility versus the overbearing, persuasion versus the inflamed, deception versus the inflamed, and authority versus the perverse.

第五节 《尉缭子·战威》
Section 5 *Power of War · Sir Weiliao*

故先王务尊于兵。尊于兵，其本有五：委积不多则事不行，赏禄不厚则民不劝，武士不选则士不强，备用不便则士不横，刑诛不必则士不畏。先王务此五者，故静能守其所有，动能成其所欲。

Therefore, ancient lords paid special attention to five aspects of warfare: people are enervated if provisions are inadequate; soldiers are discouraged if rewards and pay are insufficient; troops are weak if recruitment is not based on valiance; the army is not effective if it is ill-equipped; there is no awe or submission if rewarding and punishment are improper. With these five one can hold a solid position in defenses and achieve victories in operations.

第六节 《国语·越语下》
Section 6 *Remarks of Yüeh · Remarks of the States*

夫勇者，逆德也；兵者，凶器也；争者，事之末也。阴谋逆德，好用凶器，始于人者，人之所卒也；淫佚之事，上帝之禁也，先行此者，不利。

Aggression runs counter to virtue. Therefore, weapons are ominous tools, and fighting the last resort. He who harbors a motive for war or conspires to start a war is doomed. Heaven forbids the thirst for war and he who starts a war is cursed.

第九章　佛家
Chapter IX　Buddhism

第一节　《菩提本无树》
Section 1　*There's Nothing Like a Boddhi Tree*

身是菩提树，
心如明镜台，
时时勤拂拭，
勿使惹尘埃。
My body is a Bodhi tree,
My heart is like a mirror stand.
I clean it to make it speck-free,
So that dust has nowhere to land.

菩提本无树，
明镜亦非台。
本来无一物，
何处惹尘埃。
There's nothing like a Bodhi tree,
Nor such thing as a mirror stand.
There is nothing that you might see.
Where can dust find a place to land?

第二节 《无量寿经·歌叹佛德》

Section 2 *The Great Merits of Buddha · The Immortal Buddha*

彼国菩萨，承佛威神，于一食顷，复往十方无边净刹，供养诸佛。华香幢幡，供养之具，应念即至，皆现手中。珍妙殊特，非世所有，以奉诸佛及菩萨众。其所散华，即于空中，合为一华，华皆向下。端圆周匝，化成华盖，百千光色，色色异香，香气普熏。盖之小者，满十由旬，如是转倍，乃至遍覆三千大千世界。随其前后，以次化没。若不更以新华重散，前所散华终不复落。于虚空中共奏天乐，以微妙音歌叹佛德。经须臾间，还其本国，都悉集会七宝讲堂。无量寿佛，则为广宣大教，演畅妙法。莫不欢喜，心解得道。即时香风吹七宝树，出五音声。无量妙华，随风四散，自然供养，如是不绝。一切诸天，皆赍百千华香，万种伎乐，供养彼佛，及诸菩萨声闻之众。前后往来，熙怡快乐。此皆无量寿佛本愿加威，及曾供养如来，善根相续，无缺减故，善修习故，善摄取故，善成就故。

The Bodhisattva from that land, empowered by the Amitabha Buddha, within a meal time, went to, and back from, the ten-direction boundless Pure Land to serve the Buddhas. Flowers, incenses, banners and other offerings would come to hand immediately from his mind. These offerings, exquisite, peculiar and unworldly, were dedicated to the Buddhas and Bodhisattvas. The flowers scattered in the air were immediately turned into one. The flowers were upside down, and the top of the flower was perfectly round, which was transformed into a canopy, with hundreds of lights and thousands of colors, each of which gave off different perfumes and perfumed the air. A small canopy, about a hundred and ten square kilometers large, doubled its size like this until large enough to cover three thousand big worlds. All of these flowers appeared and vanished, one after another; if no more flowers were scattered, the flowers presented would not drop any more. The Bodhisattvas played an ensemble of heavenly music, which reverberated in the void, eulogizing the great merits of the Buddha with its ethereal sound. It took only a moment for the Bodhisattvas to return to Bliss. They all gathered in the Hall of Seven Treasures, where the Immortal Buddha preached the scriptures so beautifully that the Bodhisattvas were elated and enlightened. At this time, a fragrant wind blew seven precious trees to produce five notes of music while countless wonderful flowers were scattered to the wind. Such a wonderful scene appeared time and again. All beings from Heaven carried here a hundred thousand kinds of flowers and fine incenses and played ten thousand musical instruments, singing or dancing, dedicated to the Amitabha Buddha and to the Bodhisattvas. They all went back and forth, bustling, happy and elated. That was because the Immortal Buddha had supported them, and the goodness of serving the Tathagata had continued without decrease and because they were good at cultivation, good at digestion and good at completion.

第三节　《四十二章经》
Section 3　*The Buddha's Fourty-two Sutras*

佛言："有人患淫不止，欲自断阴。佛谓之曰：'若断其阴，不如断心。心如功曹，功曹若止，从者都息。邪心不止，断阴何益？'"

佛为说偈：欲生于汝意，意以思想生，二心各寂静，非色亦非行。

佛言："此偈是迦叶佛说。"

Buddha said: "There was one who had excessive lust and would cut his penis off." Buddha told him: "You'd rather cut off your heart than your penis. Your heart is the leader; if the leader stops, all followers stop. If your lustful heart does not stop, what's the use of cutting off your penis?" Buddha gave him a gatha: Your lust is from your avarice, and your avarice from your thought; without lust or avarice, your heart calms down, no more disturbances or anxieties. Buddha said: "This gatha is from Kashyapa."

佛言："夫为道者，如牛负重。行深泥中，疲极不敢左右顾视；出离淤泥，乃可苏息。沙门当观情欲，甚于淤泥。直心念道，可免苦矣！"

Buddha said: "He who practices the Word is like an ox carrying a heavy pack, walking in deep mud, exhausted, not daring to look aside. Only when he is out of the mud can he have a rest. Sramana, you should guard against your lust more than mud, focused on the Word with your heart so as to be free of pains."

第四节 《阿弥陀经》
Section 4 *Amitabha Sutras*

尔时，佛告长老舍利弗："从是西方，过十万亿佛土有世界名曰极乐。其土有佛，号阿弥陀，今现在说法。舍利弗，彼土何故名为极乐？其国众生，无有众苦，但受诸乐，故名极乐。又舍利弗，极乐国土，七重栏楯，七重罗网，七重行树，皆是四宝周匝围绕，是故彼国名为极乐。又舍利弗，极乐国土，有七宝池，八功德水，充满其中。池底纯以金沙布地。四边阶道，金、银、琉璃、玻璃合成。上有楼阁，亦以金、银、琉璃、玻璃、砗磲、赤珠、玛瑙而严饰之。池中莲华大如车轮，青色青光，黄色黄光，赤色赤光，白色白光，微妙香洁。舍利弗，极乐国土，成就如是功德庄严。又舍利弗，彼佛国土，常作天乐，黄金为地。昼夜六时，雨天曼陀罗华。其土众生，常以清旦，各以衣裓盛众妙华，供养他方十万亿佛。即以食时，还到本国，饭食经行。舍利弗，极乐国土，成就如是功德庄严。复次舍利弗，彼国常有种种奇妙杂色之鸟：白鹤、孔雀、鹦鹉、舍利、迦陵频伽、共命之鸟。是诸众鸟，昼夜六时，出和雅音。其音演畅五根、五力、七菩提分、八圣道分，如是等法。其土众生，闻是音已，皆悉念佛、念法、念僧。舍利弗，汝勿谓此鸟实是罪报所生。所以者何？彼佛国土，无三恶道。舍利弗，其佛国土，尚无恶道之名，何况有实？是诸众鸟，皆是阿弥陀佛欲令法音宣流，变化所作。舍利弗，彼佛国土，微风吹动诸宝行树及宝罗网，出微妙音，譬如百千种乐同时俱作。闻是音者，自然皆生念佛、念法、念僧之心。舍利弗，其佛国土，成就如是功德庄严。”

Then the Buddha told the Elder Sariputra: “After 10 trillion Buddha worlds west from here, there is a world called Bliss. And there, there is a Buddha, Amitabha by name. He is still preaching now! Sariputra, why is that land called Bliss? Because in that land all beings, free of all pains, enjoy various pleasures, hence it is called Bliss. Besides, Sariputra, Bliss is enclosed by seven rows of railings, seven rows of nets and seven rows of trees, all made of four kinds of jewels, hence it is named Bliss. Besides, Sariputra, in the Land of Bliss, there is a pond of seven treasures, filled with water of eight merits. The bottom of the pond is spread with gold sand, and around the pool are stairways made of gold, silver, glaze and crystal. Up there stand towers adorned with gold, silver, glaze, glass, giant clam shells, red pearls and agate. In the pond are the lotus flowers as large as wheels, the blue emitting blue light, the yellow emitting yellow light, the red emitting red light, and the white emitting white light, so subtle, fragrant and clean. Sariputra, the Land of Bliss is complete with such meritorious grandeur! Besides, Sariputra, the Buddha Land often rings with celestial music, the ground covered with gold. And there are showers of Mandarava flowers day and night. The beings on the land often rise early in the morning and carry the wondrous flowers with their skirts to make sacrifices to 10 trillion Buddhas from other places. By breakfast time, they’ve returned to their own land to have a meal followed by a meditation. Sariputra, the Land of Bliss is blessed with such virtue and splendor! Furthermore, Sariputra, in that land one can often see various birds of variegated feathers, such as white cranes, peacocks, parrots, sariras, kalavinkas and common-fate birds. Such birds warble with elegance day and night, preaching Five Roots, Five Forces, Seven Bodhi Twigs, Eight Holy Ways, so and so forth. Hearing such news, all beings on the land turn their mind to chant Buddha, Dharma and Sangha. Sariputra, don’t think that these birds were born out of retributions. Why? On that Buddha Land there are no such things as Three Sins. Sariputra, on that Buddha Land there are not even names of sins, let alone facts. All those birds answer Amitabha's call to circulate and translate Dharma. Sariputra, on that Buddha Land a breeze blows all jeweled trees and jeweled nets to produce vivid subtle sounds as if thousands of melodies are played simultaneously. Those who hear the sounds naturally give their heart to Buddha, to Dharma, and to Sangha. Sariputra, that Buddha Land is complete with such virtue and splendor!"

第五节 《法句经·序》
Section 5 Preface to *Dharmapada*

又诸佛典，皆在天竺。天竺言语与汉异音。云其书为天书，语为天语，名物不同，传实不易。唯昔蓝调、安侯世高、都尉、弗调，译胡为汉，审得其体，斯以难继。后之传者，虽不能密，尤尚贵其实，粗得大趣。始者维祇难出自天竺，以黄武三年来适武昌。仆从受此五百偈本，请其同道竺将炎为译。将炎虽善天竺语，未备晓汉，其所传言，或得胡语，或以义出音，近于质直。仆初嫌其辞不雅，维祇难曰："佛言依其义不用饰，取其法不以严。其传经者，当令易晓，勿失厥义，是则为善。"座中咸曰："老氏称'美言不信，信言不美。'仲尼亦云：'书不尽言，言不尽意'。明圣人意深邃无极。今传胡义，实宜径达。"是以自竭，受译人口，因循本旨，不加文饰。译所不解，则阙不传。故有脱失，多不出者。

All Buddhist s are from India. The language of India is different from Chinese. It's said their books are cryptic, and their language is cryptic, too. As things and names are different, it's surely hard to translate them. Of old, Lantiao, Anhou, Shikao, Tuwei and Fotiao translated Sanskrit into Chinese so appropriately that very few could follow suit. Later translators, unable to be exact, laid emphasis on facts and managed to get main ideas. A man called Vighna from India came to Wuch'ang at the third year of Huangwu. He gave me

500 books of Buddhist sutras. I asked his colleague called Chiangyan Chu to translate them. Although Chiangyan was good at the language of India, he was not necessarily versed in Chinese. So in his translation there were Sanskrit expressions either literally rendered or simply transliterated, too literal I would say. I dislike his work for lack of elegance in the first place. Vighna argued: “The translation of Buddha’s words should be adherent to the meaning, disregarding rhetoric, and we should retain its Dharma, free of rigidity. Those who translate should stress on transparency without losing the original meaning, hence good translations.” Those who were present all claimed, “Laocius said: ‘Beautiful words are not faithful and faithful words are not beautiful’. And Confucius said: ‘Words fail a book, senses fail a form’. What a saint says is the profound of the profoundest. In translating sutras, just express the content.” Therefore, when translating sutras, follow the original import without using ornate words. If sutras are not well translated, they won’t last long; If some message is missing in the original, a translator does not have to make it up.”

参考文献
References

[1] 诗经. 王秀梅，译注. 北京：中华书局，2016.

[2] 楚辞. 林家骊，译注. 2 版. 北京：中华书局，2015.

[3] 文心雕龙. 王志彬，译注. 北京：中华书局，2012.

[4] [唐]李白. 李太白全集. [清]王琦，注. 北京：中华书局，2015.

[5] [唐]杜甫. 杜诗详注. [清] 仇兆鳌，注. 北京：中华书局，2015.

[6] 左传. 郭丹，程小青，李彬源，译注. 北京：中华书局，2012.

[7] [汉]司马迁. 史记. 韩兆琦，评注. 长沙：岳麓书社，2011.

[8] [汉]班固. 汉书. 北京：中华书局，2007.

[9] [唐]吴兢. 贞观政要. 骈宇骞，骈骅，译. 北京：中华书局，2009.

[10] 张宏儒，沈志华. 资治通鉴：文白对照全译. 北京：改革出版社，1991.

[11] 周易. 郭彧，译注. 北京：中华书局，2012.

[12] 尚书. 王世舜，王翠叶，译注. 北京：中华书局，2012.

[13] 论语. 陈晓芬，译注. 北京：中华书局，2011.

[14] 孟子译注. 杨伯峻，译注. 北京：中华书局，2010.

[15] 胡平生，译注. 孝经译注. 北京：中华书局，1999.

[16] [清]黄元吉. 道德经注释. 蒋门马，校注. 北京：中华书局，2012.

[17] 庄子. 方勇，译注. 2 版. 北京：中华书局，2015.

[18] 墨子. 方勇，译注. 2 版. 北京：中华书局，2015.

[19] 韩非子. 高华平，王齐洲，张三夕，译. 北京：中华书局，2014.

[20] 孙子兵法. 陈曦，译注. 北京：中华书局，2011.

[21] 银雀山汉墓竹简整理小组. 孙膑兵法. 北京：文物出版社，1975.

[22] 兵经百字 唐李问对. 戴庞海，阎睿，周媛，译注. 郑州：中州古籍出版社，2010.
[23] 尉缭子 吴子. 徐勇，注译. 郑州：中州古籍出版社，2010.
[24] 国语. 陈桐生，译注. 北京：中华书局，2013.
[25] [梁]释僧佑. 出三藏记集. 北京：中华书局，1995.
[26] 饶宗颐. 六祖坛经. 北京：中信出版社，2013.
[27] 无量寿经. 陈林，译注. 北京：中华书局，2010.
[28] 四十二章经. 尚荣，译注. 北京：中华书局，2010.
[29] 阿弥陀经. 王党辉 ，译注. 郑州：中州古籍出版社，2010.
[30] 赵彦春. 诗经英译. 北京：外文出版社，2016.
[31] 赵彦春. 道德经英译. 北京：高等教育出版社，2018.
[32] 赵彦春. 论语英译. 北京：高等教育出版社，2018.
[33] 赵彦春. 庄子英译. 北京：高等教育出版社，2019.
[34] 赵彦春. 李白诗歌全集英译. 上海：上海大学出版社，2020.
[35] 赵彦春. 杜甫诗歌英译. 上海：上海大学出版社，2021.
[36] 赵彦春. 屈原楚辞英译. 上海：上海大学出版社，2022.